Europe and the Constitution after Maastricht

by
Martin Howe

ISBN 1-874607-04-4

Published by Nelson & Pollard
Oxford

The Author

Martin Howe is a barrister specialising in intellectual property law and European Community law. He is a former Conservative Parliamentary candidate and is a leading member of the Society of Conservative Lawyers.

This paper was originally published by the Society of Conservative Lawyers in June 1992: it went to press before the Danish referendum result. The paper has been revised and updated to take account of the tumultuous events since then, and new sections have been added on monetary union, the "intergovernmental" parts of Maastricht, European citizenship, and "ever closer union" and the Maastricht Treaty revision due in 1996.

ISBN 1-874607-04-4

© Copyright Martin Howe 1992, 1993

Published by Nelson & Pollard

Table of Contents

Chapter 1   Introduction   1

Chapter 2   European Community Law and National Laws   3

    2.1 European Institutions and Sources of Law   3

    2.2 Community Law in the United Kingdom   8

Chapter 3   Examples of Community Law in Practice   13

    3.1 Sex Equality at Work   13

    3.2 Factortame and the Suspension of Acts of Parliament   18

    3.3 Sunday Trading and Europe   22

    3.4 Border Controls and the Internal Market   26

Chapter 4   Principles of Development of the EEC   29

    4.1 Can Sovereignty be "Pooled"?   29

    4.2 The role of the European Court of Justice   33

    4.3 "Federalism" and the importance of general words   37

Chapter 5   The Treaty of Maastricht   41

    5.1 Outline of the Treaty   41

    5.2 "Subsidiarity" in theory and in practice   43

    5.3 Maastricht and "intergovernmentalism"   50

    5.4 Citizenship of the European Union   52

    5.5 Monetary Union and the UK's "opt-out"   54

    5.6 Maastricht and the Social Charter   57

Chapter 6   The Way Ahead   61

    6.1 Protecting the British Constitution   61

    6.2 "Ever closer union" and the 1996 Treaty revision   64

    6.3 What happens if Maastricht is not ratified?   66

    6.4 Promoting a Europe of Nation States   67

Notes   71

Chapter 1

Introduction

Thanks to the Treaty of Maastricht – or the Treaty on European Union, to give it its official title – the debate about Britain's future in Europe has become a major part of domestic politics. It has ceased to be the minority interest which it once was.

But there are two parts to the debate about Europe: first, disagreement about ultimate objectives, and, secondly, disagreement at a more factual level about the effects and consequences of developments in the European Communities. The facts have become obscured in the heat of debate about the objectives.

There has been a tendency amongst "pro-European" and government circles, to play down and seek to minimise the likely extent to which each further development in the European Communities would lead to the expansion of powers in Brussels and the diminution of the powers of Britain to regulate its affairs as a nation state. On the other hand, some committed "anti-Europeans" have on occasion overstated the consequences of Community developments. Where does the truth lie?

I am a firm believer in examining the facts first and forming opinions second. I believe that very many people in this country wish for more information, so that they can then form an intelligent view, rather than just hearing more arguments. This is my main aim in this paper.

What of my own perspective? I believe that the terms "pro-European" and "anti-European" are misleading. A particular viewpoint about what is the best form of political organisation for Europe, and Britain's relationship with it, does not mean that one is "pro" or "anti" Europe as such.

I campaigned whole-heartedly for a "Yes" vote in the 1975 common market referendum campaign. However, I do not see Britain's future as a unit in a new European super-State. The European Communities can confer great benefits: the economic benefits of the single market, and

1

the political benefits of more harmonious relationships between the peoples of Europe. However, for reasons which will become apparent from later chapters, I am increasingly concerned that current developments in Europe are undermining those economic benefits and, even more importantly, will lead to conflict rather than harmony because decisions over ever larger and more important aspects of national life will be made by European bodies which the people of individual nations cannot control.

I am a Conservative and this paper is written from a Conservative viewpoint. In some later chapters I express concern that certain policies which I, as a Conservative, would wish to follow, have been effectively removed from the power of the British Parliament and people to follow if they choose to do so. But the basic point is the same whatever one's party affiliation, even if the particular policies one wants to follow would be different.

Chapter 2

European Community Law and National Laws

2.1 European Institutions and Sources of Law

"This Treaty is more than an agreement which merely creates mutual obligations between the contracting states. This view is confirmed by the preamble to the Treaty which refers not only to governments but to peoples.... the Community constitutes a new legal order in international law for whose benefit the states have limited their sovereign rights, albeit within limited fields, and the subjects of which comprise not only the Member States but also their nationals."

The European Court of Justice in *Van Gend en Loos*.[1]

There are in fact not one, but three, "European Communities". Since however all three "Communities" have the same membership of 12 member states, and are served by the same common institutions of Commission, Council of Ministers, Parliament and Court, their separate existence is more of a legal fiction than a reality.

The oldest of the three Communities is the European Coal and Steel Community or "ECSC", which was established by the Treaty of Paris in 1951. Although, as its name implies, its scope was limited to creating a common market in the coal and steel industries, it formed the model or forerunner for by far the most important of the three Communities: the European Economic Community or "EEC", which was established by the Treaty of Rome in 1957, with the aim of creating a common market in all trade in goods and progressively approximating the economic policies of its original six Member States.

The third European Community, also established in 1957, is only of specialist interest: it is the European Atomic Energy Community, or "Euratom".

The European Communities have been progressively expanded from their original six Member States to 12 today; the United Kingdom joined the European Communities on 1st January 1973.

The European Economic Community was established, as its name suggests, as a primarily economic body: to create a customs union and a common market between its Member States, and for related economic purposes. Its purposes are now far wider than merely economic, and as a result a practice has grown up referring to it as the European Community simpliciter or "EC", the "Economic" having been dropped. The Maastricht Treaty, once it is ratified, will formally drop the word "Economic" from the name of the EEC.[2]

The creation of a common market and customs union implies that its Member States must necessarily accept certain restrictions upon the freedom of action which they would otherwise enjoy, if only to prevent Member States imposing barriers or unfair disadvantages against goods from other Member States. As a matter of legal mechanics, such restrictions could perhaps be made to operate solely at the level of relations between states as Treaty provisions. These, as a matter of **international** law, bind the states which are parties to them.

The Treaty of Rome, however, does not simply act as a Treaty between member states at the level of international law; it requires that its provisions, and many very important regulations and decisions by Community institutions established under the Treaty, be incorporated as part of the internal laws of all the Member States.[3] Thus, the Treaty and subordinate Community legislation are made binding directly upon businesses and private individuals within the Member States; and may also be used to challenge the governmental authorities and legislatures of the Member States **under their own legal systems**.

In this respect, the EEC is fundamentally different from most other international organisations. It has been put as follows: "Thus the unique character of the Communities lies in the degree of their penetration into the internal legal relations of the Member States, whereas classical international organizations tend to be involved merely with the external legal relations of their members."[4] It is the legal and particularly the constitutional impact of this aspect of the Treaty of Rome which is the special subject of this paper.

The Treaty of Rome is more than just a Treaty and, in fact, creates a developed system of law of its own, distinct from the laws of its Member States: "Community law", which is interpreted by the European Court of Justice at Luxembourg ("ECJ").

The sources of such "Community" law begin with the Treaty of Rome and the other Community Treaties, such as the Single European Act of 1986, and, once ratified, the Treaty of Maastricht. The Treaties contain the most important rules of Community law, define the powers of the Community institutions, and provide the constitutional framework under which is made a vast further body of Community law.

This consists of regulations, directives and decisions of both the Council of Ministers and of the Commission. The Council of Ministers consists of Ministers representing the governments of each of the Member States. In fact it consists of different groups of ministers for different purposes (finance, agriculture, etc.). Decisions of the Council of Ministers are made, according to complex rules, on some questions by unanimous vote and on other questions by a weighted majority vote.[5] It is a legislative body: many of its decisions directly become law, and in this respect it is totally unlike the Cabinet in the United Kingdom which is an executive, not legislative, body. However, unlike almost every other legislature in the free world, the Council of Ministers almost invariably meets in private session.

The Commission is sometimes described (but only by the ignorant) merely as a bureaucratic body staffed by civil servants who carry out the wishes of their political masters in the Council of Ministers. Nothing could be further from the truth. The Commissioners are all politicians, not civil servants. The Commission has substantial law-making, as well as executive, powers of its own. As an institution, it has always regarded itself as the enlightened bearer of the true faith of European integration against what it sees as the backward nationalism of the Member States.[6] Even in matters outside its own law-making powers, the Commission has an important role of formulating and proposing legislation to the

Council of Ministers[7] and through this process it exerts constant pressure for extending the process of European integration.

The European Parliament, despite its name,[8] has only a limited role in the Community legislative process: it is essentially limited to consultation on proposed measures and a never-used power to dismiss the members of the Commission. Its role will be expanded by the Maastricht Treaty.

The Treaties form the primary source of law, or "constitution" of the Communities. Under the Treaties, the bulk of Community law is contained in *regulations and directives*. The Official Journal of the European Communities is filled with thousands of pages of regulations and directives every year. Both the Council of Ministers and the Commission have powers to make regulations and issue directives for a variety of purposes under the Treaties.

A regulation is legislation in the same way as an Act of the UK Parliament or a law passed by the legislature of any of the other Member States. No further act of the legislatures or governments of Member States is needed before a regulation becomes part of their domestic law: in the words of the Treaty of Rome, Art. 189(2): "A regulation shall have general application. It shall be binding in its entirety and directly applicable in all Member States."

Art. 189(3) continues: "A directive shall be binding, as to the result to be achieved, upon each Member State to which it is addressed, but shall leave to the national authorities the choice of form and methods." A directive therefore normally requires the Member States to pass national implementing legislation in order to be put into effect. At first sight, it might be thought that this provision means that a directive solely has effect as an obligation on the Member States at an international law level, and does not have direct effects as part of the legal systems of the Member States. The ECJ has however developed a doctrine of "direct effect" of directives, which means that they can frequently be relied upon before the courts of Member States.

In the real world a system of law is doubtfully described as that unless it has some effective means of enforcement. Community law is enforced by a variety of means. Regulations may sometimes be enforced by direct action by Community institutions. The most important area where this happens is in the field of competition law, where the Commission regularly arrives at decisions fining companies for operating cartels or for other breaches of Community competition rules.

Community law may also be enforced by the Commission, or other member states, taking action against a member state for a breach of Community law under Article 169 or 170 of the Treaty of Rome. The Court's decisions under these articles at the end of the day carry no sanction as such: they have the same binding effect on states as decisions of other international law tribunals and in theory at least public obloquy and World opinion will motivate a state to comply with such judgments. The Treaty of Maastricht will for the first time confer upon the Court a power to impose fines on Member States for such breaches.[9]

Of greatest practical importance however, now and even more so in the future, is the direct application of Community law through the courts of Member States. All courts and tribunals of Member States are obliged under the Treaty to apply Community law; and in the event of a conflict, to apply Community law in preference to the rules of their own national law: "A national court which is called upon ... to apply provisions of Community law is under a duty to give full effect to those provisions, if necessary refusing of its own motion to apply any conflicting provisions of national legislation, even if adopted subsequently, and it is not necessary for the court to request or await a prior setting aside of such provision by legislative or other constitutional means."[10]

Community law even claims to override the fundamental or constitutional laws of the Member States: "The law stemming from the Treaty, an independent source of law, cannot because of its very nature be overridden by rules of national law, however framed ... Therefore the validity of a Community measure or its effect within a Member State remains unimpaired even if it is alleged that it runs counter to either fundamental rights as formulated by the Constitution of that State or the principles of a national constitutional structure."[11]

Since the precise interpretation of Community law may often be a matter of doubt, a mechanism is provided under Article 177 of the Treaty for national courts to refer cases to the European Court for the interpretation of Community law. This is an appeal in all but name: although the case is then referred back to the national court for the final order or decision to be made there, the national court has no power to do other than to apply Community law as interpreted by the European Court of Justice.

The reference procedure is a very powerful instrument for the implementation of Community law within Member States. It gives the European Court of Justice a very powerful role throughout the Community, and it is therefore of crucial importance how the Court discharges that role. In particular, is the European Court an impartial umpire of the limits of Community law and of the powers of the Community institutions as laid down in the Treaties, or does it see its role differently? This subject is addressed in more depth in Chapter 4.2 below.

2.2 Community Law in the United Kingdom

"But when we come to matters with a European element, the Treaty is like an incoming tide. It flows into the estuaries and up the rivers. It cannot be held back."   Lord Denning MR in *Bulmer.*[12]

"Community" law, as already described, is a self-contained system of law derived from the Treaties and the institutions created under them. Community law claims to be a higher order of law than the national laws of the Member States and to prevail over all the national laws which are inconsistent with it. But from where does that system of Community law derive its force, so that judges in the courts of the United Kingdom are obliged to follow and give effect to it?

Under the constitution of the United Kingdom, unlike that of some other countries,[13] treaties as such do not have any force as law in the domestic courts of the United Kingdom. They are executive acts of the Crown, not legislative acts, and as such, although they are binding on the Crown as a matter of **international** law, the domestic courts of the United Kingdom will not enforce them. Compliance or non-compliance with treaties is normally purely a matter for the Crown in the exercise of its prerogative powers to regulate the external relations of the United Kingdom. The sole sanction for non-compliance with international law obligations is pressure from other States, coupled in some circumstances with decisions of international courts or arbitral bodies which create a moral pressure for compliance.

In order for Treaties to have effect as part of the internal law of the United Kingdom, there must be an Act of Parliament giving them the force of law. Accordingly in 1972 the European Communities Act was passed in order to allow the United Kingdom to accede to the European Communities. The Act gives effect to Community law through section 2(1), which reads:

"2(1). All such rights, powers, liabilities, obligations and restrictions from time to time created or arising by or under the Treaties, and all such remedies and procedures from time to time provided by or under the Treaties, as in accordance with the Treaties are without further enactment to be given legal effect or used in the United Kingdom shall be recognised and available in law, and be enforced, allowed and followed accordingly;"

The effect of the 1972 Act is that all the courts of this country must give direct effect to Community law. They may be aided in this task by references to the European Court of Justice in Luxembourg, and its interpretation of the Treaties or other Community instruments is effectively final: European Communities Act 1972, section 3(1):

"3(1). For the purposes of legal proceedings any question as to the meaning or effect of any of the Treaties, or as to the validity, meaning or effect of any Community instrument shall be treated as a question of law ... and before determination as such in accordance with the principles laid down by and any relevant decision of the European Court."

This leaves the question of what happens if a conflict arises between national and Community law. In such circumstances, where does the duty of the judge lie? To apply Community law, or to apply the law of his own national Parliament? An answer, although not a complete one, is to be found in section 2(4) of the 1972 Act:

" ... any enactment passed or to be passed, other than one contained in this Part of this Act, shall be construed and have effect subject to the foregoing provisions of this section;"

The "foregoing provisions of this section" of course include subsection 2(1), quoted above.

The position is straightforward where there is a conflict between a later Community law and an earlier Act of Parliament, or between Community law and a subordinate instrument such as an Order in Council or ministerial regulation: in such a case, Community law will prevail.

The question is more vexed if a conflict arises between a provision of Community law and a **later** Act of Parliament. In such a case has Parliament, by enacting the later Act, effectively revoked the authority which it gave under the European Communities Act 1972 for the inconsistent provision of Community law to be recognised as part of the law of the United Kingdom? Or is Parliament now incapable of revoking that authority even if it wishes to do so?

The position is affected not only by the terms of the European Communities Act 1972, but also by the fundamental constitutional doctrine of the United Kingdom, "the sovereignty of Parliament". Under this doctrine, there are no limits on the power of Parliament, but it cannot bind its successor. Thus, any limitation purportedly imposed by an earlier Parliament on its powers can be overturned by a successor Parliament.

The interaction between Community law, the 1972 Act, and the doctrine of the sovereignty of Parliament, has given rise to considerable academic debate. At one extreme, it has been suggested that the European Communities Act 1972 has created a wholly new constitutional order which has superseded the sovereignty of Parliament;[14] this would imply that were Parliament now consciously and deliberately to disapply Community law in whole or in part, thereby repealing the European Communities Act 1972, then it would be impossible to do so: a Court in the United Kingdom would have to hold the new Act of Parliament void, and the present day Parliament effectively bound by the Parliament of 1972.

The general consensus of academic opinion is that the traditional sovereignty of Parliament has not been abrogated that far, and that although the 1972 Act would have the effect of rendering void any provisions of Acts of Parliament which are unintentionally contrary to Community law, an Act which expressly said that it superseded Community law would prevail.

Thus, the approach is one of divining the intention of Parliament as expressed in the later Act. If the later Act says nothing expressly about conflicts with Community law then it is to be interpreted as if a section were written into it, saying that its provisions were to be subject to any directly enforceable Community rights given effect under section 2(1) of the European Communities Act 1972.[15] The implication of this approach would appear to be that if Parliament does make it expressly clear, by stating in terms, that a new Act is to prevail over section 2(1) of the European Communities Act 1972 and so prevail over Community law deriving force thereunder, then the new Act will prevail as part of the law of the United Kingdom.

It is, however, on this kind of fundamental question that a drift of judicial opinion can occur over time: doctrines accepted today may in the future reach the stage of no longer being accepted, not because they have been expressly altered or abrogated by a specific piece of legislation or legal act, but because of a general change of climate. How far does the continuing process of European integration have to go before the courts of the United Kingdom express the view that there has been a change to a wholly new constitutional order which has superseded the sovereignty of Parliament, and under which Parliament is, **as part of the law of the United Kingdom**, subordinate to the Treaties?

Whether or not there is in the immediately foreseeable future any real likelihood that Parliament might wish to abrogate the effect of Community law in the United Kingdom in whole or in part, it must be a matter of some concern that so fundamental a question as Parliament's ultimate right to take that step is potentially in sufficient doubt to have become a matter of academic and judicial debate. The existence of an ultimate right of secession, even if arguably theoretical, is after all the ultimate touchstone of the continued existence of the sovereignty of a nation state. A combination of states which, under their own internal constitution, must give precedence to the central laws of the combination and have lost the right to reject or modify those laws is, under whatever definition one chooses to apply, truly "federal".

Because of the political debate then taking place over the entry of the United Kingdom into the Common Market, there were no doubt good reasons for the sensitive subject of conflict between Community law and Acts of Parliament to have been dealt with in an inexplicit way in the drafting of the European Communities Act 1972. However, given the present state and the likely future development of the European Communities, there could be a strong case for the precise constitutional position of Community law in the United Kingdom now to be spelled out in a clearer way: with explicit conflict rules to apply in the event of inconsistencies between Community law and prior and subsequent Acts of Parliament and subordinate legislation, and with the clear enshrinement of Parliament's ultimate authority, as a matter of the law of the United Kingdom, to decide whether or not and, if so, to what extent, rules of Community law are to be given force within the United Kingdom. I return to this subject in Chapter 6.1 below.

Chapter 3

Examples of Community Law in Practice

3.1 Sex Equality at Work

To what extent is equality for women in one member state a matter of legitimate concern in other member states, or to the central European institutions? No doubt in all civilised societies today, and in particular in European societies, the general principle of social and economic equality between the sexes is accepted. But there are many ways of implementing that general principle, and it is far from obvious that it should be necessary to adopt a uniform approach at a level of detail in all Member States.

The relevant part of the Treaty of Rome, Article 119, part of the Treaty's Social Provisions, is fairly general in its terms:

"Each Member State shall during the first stage ensure and subsequently maintain the principle that men and women should receive equal pay for equal work."

It is worth making three obvious points about this provision of the Treaty. First, it states a "principle", which is to be maintained by Member States. On the face of it, this "principle" does not claim to be a rule of law. Secondly, it refers only to "equal pay", not to other forms of discrimination such as different retiring ages. Thirdly, it refers to "equal work", not to **different** work which may or may not arguably be of "equal value".

This Treaty provision was considered by the ECJ in the leading case of *Defrenne v. SABENA*[16], in which an air stewardess employed by Belgian airlines complained of unequal treatment on the ground of sex. The Court held that Article 119 was directly applicable as part of the law of the Member States, and that it could be relied upon by individuals before the courts of Member States "as regards those types of discrimination arising directly from legislative provisions or collective labour agreements, as well as in cases in which men and women receive unequal pay for equal work."[17] But the Court added a rider to its decision to the effect that the direct effect of Article 119 could not be relied upon "in order to support claims concerning pay periods prior to the date of this judgment, except as regards those workers who have already brought legal proceedings or made an equivalent claim."[18]

The court's decision that the "principle" in Article 119 was directly applicable in member states as a rule of Community law, was a matter of some surprise at the time. What, however, is legally and jurisprudentially quite startling about the decision of the Court is the qualification added to its decision, whereby it directed that Article 119 could be so relied upon only for the future. If the Court was right that Article 119 was directly applicable, then it **had** formed part of the laws of Member States, according to the Court's reasoning, from 1st January 1962 onwards in the original Six Member States.

Having found, as a matter of interpretation of the Treaty, that the workers of the Six had enjoyed a directly enforceable Community right to equal pay, by what power did the Court direct that that right should not be enforced, making a limited exception of dubious fairness in the cases of workers who had already filed claims? The plain answer is that the Court had no such power. This part of the Court's decision was manifestly a legislative act, not a judicial act.

The Treaty confers no legislative power on the Court.[19] Article 164 states that "The Court of Justice shall ensure that in the interpretation and application of this Treaty the law is observed." The question then arises, that if the Court itself departs from the bounds of its lawful powers, who is there to ensure that the Court itself observes the law?

Apart from the jurisprudential objection to this part of the decision, it, like a clock striking 13, casts doubt upon what goes before. If the Court was confident of the correctness of its decision that Article 119 was as a matter of interpretation directly applicable, then why shouldn't it apply as from the date when it formed part of the law? The whole of the Court's decision can therefore be more properly regarded as a legislative rather than a judicial act: legislating in effect that **henceforth**, Article 119 shall form part of directly applicable Community law.

As stated above, Art 119 of the Treaty refers to equal pay, not to other forms of discrimination in employment terms, such as differing retirement ages, and this interpretation was initially confirmed by the ECJ.[20] In doing so, however, the ECJ stated that:

"respect for fundamental personal human rights is one of the general principles of Community law, the observance of which the Court has a duty to ensure. There can be no doubt that the elimination of discrimination based on sex forms part of those fundamental rights."[21]

In the later case of *Barber v. Guardian Royal Exchange*,[22] the ECJ significantly broadened its definition of "pay" for the purposes of Article 119. It held that "pay" included redundancy terms and privately-funded pension payments, with the consequence that differences in redundancy and pension entitlements consequent upon different retirement ages of the sexes were contrary to Community law. In this case, it was a man rather than a woman who succeeded in a claim. The Court added a "prospective effect only" rider to its decision, similar to the one it had added in the *Defrenne v. SABENA* case. The Court, perhaps acknowledging the unexpected nature of its decision, added that "the parties concerned were reasonably entitled to consider that Article 119 did not apply to pensions paid out under contracted-out schemes ... ".[23]

The implications of this decision were profound, threatening to add hugely and unexpectedly to the liabilities of the occupational pension industry and of employers. Despite the "no retrospective effect" rider to the Court's decision, it caused severe uncertainties as to the precise scope of employers' liabilities to make payments in order to equalise pension provisions.

Quite apart from the efforts of the European Court in this field, the obligations of Member States as regards sex equality under the Treaty have been extended by a number of directives, the most important of which are Council Directive 75/117[24] on equal pay, Council Directive 76/207[25] on equal treatment in access to employment, training and working conditions, Council Directive 79/7[26] on social security, and Council Directive 86/378[27] on occupational pensions and other benefits.

It is worth noting that the first two of these Directives were adopted during the term of office of the last Labour government and have caused repeated problems of conflict with the employment policies of the Conservative government. The later wishes of the British people, democratically expressed at four successive General Elections, have been for a Conservative and therefore a free-market approach to economic management. However, the mechanics of the Community legislative process render it impossible for these Directives to be amended into a less interventionist form, still less revoked, without the unanimous or near-unanimous agreement of the other Member States, which would certainly not be forthcoming. We see here the operation of a ratchet effect, where legislation once agreed cannot later be reversed, despite a profound change after 1979 in the democratically expressed will of the British people.

Together, these Directives form an extensive code covering all aspects of employment, all the way from selection for employment, through training and promotion, pay and working conditions, to pensions and other social security benefits, both public and private. The approach to be applied is laid down in considerable detail. One aspect worth considering is the concept of equal pay for work of "equal value".

As stated above, Article 119 of the Treaty in terms only refers to equal pay for "equal work". However, as part of its judgment in the *SABENA* case[28] the European Court made reference to extending "the narrow criterion of 'equal work', in accordance in particular with the provisions of International Labour Organisation Convention No. 100, Article 2 which establishes the principle of equal pay for work 'of equal value'." This principle, of work of "equal value", involves attempting to compare in some way two jobs which are different from each other in order to establish whether or not they are of equal "value".

A whole host of questions arise: in comparing the work involved in two jobs, does one look only at the intrinsic nature of the work and the skills involved, or does one look at market factors such as the shortage of suitably qualified workers to do one, but not the other, of the jobs? If one ignores the market factor, what meaning does "value" have in the absence of a market which establishes pay levels? These problems arise for example (in a real case) comparing the "value" of the work done by a welder with the work done in food preparation in a canteen.

Without entering into the details of the economic arguments involved, it is clear that there is considerable scope for legitimate differences of view about the questions: to what extent does a principle of equal pay for "equal work" require to be extended to different work considered to be of "equal value"? If so, what is the precise manner in which "equal value" is to be assessed and compared? It might be thought that these are questions upon which the different Member States, having regard to their differing employment practices and cultures, might legitimately implement the general principle in a variety of different ways.

Yet we can see here in the progression of events the way in which what started as a very general Treaty provision – indeed, a Treaty provision avowedly only stating a "principle" – has led inexorably to the compulsory adoption of detailed rules applying uniformly to all Member States and laying down a very particular and precise form of "equal pay" for work of allegedly "equal value". The "principle" has furthermore been extended outside the terms stated by the Treaty to other non-pay aspects of employment terms such as pension ages.

The question must be asked whether an impartial observer of events who looked at the text of the Treaty of Rome when it was signed, or indeed when the United Kingdom acceded at the beginning of 1973, would have foreseen the way in which this principle would be interpreted, applied and developed into the present state of affairs. If not, it must be asked whether the Community institutions are truly engaged in implementing the Treaties in accordance with their terms, or whether their role has gone beyond that.

Having looked at how this general principle in the Treaty has been worked through in practice into the laws of the United Kingdom and the other Member States, it is worth asking the even more fundamental question of why a provision of this kind is found at all in a Treaty establishing a common market. Is it really necessary for the functioning of the common market for the Community to venture into the field of social policy? How does the application of Community law in the social field square with the principle of "subsidiarity" discussed in Chapter 5.2

below, under which only decisions which **need to** be taken in common at Community level should be taken at that level?

Article 119 forms part of Title III of the Treaty, entitled "Social Policy". The reality is that the Social Policy provisions of the Treaty were seen as a "goody" which could be presented as a "benefit" to be provided by Europe to the people of the Member States, in contrast to the common market and customs union which were seen as a benefit to businesses. This is, of course, an outdated viewpoint nowadays even in socialist or social democratic circles, treating the interests of businesses and of people as if they were diametrically opposed. Of course it is illusory to speak of a "benefit" coming from "Europe": Europe does not pay for the benefits, whose cost falls on businesses or governments of member states.

The compulsory enactment of these provisions in Community law confers no benefit: all the Member States are free, if that is their democratic wish, to implement such benefits under their own laws. Making them the subject of compulsory and uniform regulation at Community level merely serves to reduce the scope for democratic freedom of action of Member States in the social sphere.

3.2 Factortame and the Suspension of Acts of Parliament

"Whereas the late King ... did endeavour to subvert ... the laws and liberties of this kingdome ... by assumeing and exerciseing a power of dispensing with and suspending of lawes and the execution of lawes without the consent of Parlyament ... That the pretended power of suspending of lawes or the execution of lawes by regall authoritie as it hath been assumed and exercised of late is illegall." Bill of Rights 1688

"Factortame" is a meaningless combination of two words. Company formation agents churn out such meaningless combination words in their thousands when giving names to their "off the shelf" companies. Such companies can be bought for under £200, and need have no assets, but the law confers upon them the important advantages both of limited liability and of being regarded as a legal "person" distinct from the personality of the company's shareholders or directors.

Real companies formed to engage in real businesses usually have real names; names which describe the business or the people who are running it. Factortame Limited was an artificial legal person registered in England and therefore, in the eyes of the law, English. However, in substance and reality it was Spanish not English. It and a large number of similar companies were formed and operated by Spanish interests so that their fishing vessels could be registered as British ships and fish against the United Kingdom's fishing quota in the North Atlantic.

It might be thought that in an ideal world, a common European fisheries policy would involve the unrestricted right of all fishing vessels from Member States to fish in the waters of all other Member States. However, the need to protect fisheries from over-fishing, and at the same time to preserve the economic viability of traditional fishing industries and the communities dependent upon them, has rendered such a policy impractical. Accordingly, the Common Fisheries Policy of the EEC is based upon a system of national quotas for fishery catches.[29]

Community law in general prohibits discrimination by Member States on the ground of nationality against citizens of other members: Treaty of Rome, article 7(1). However, the creation of a fishery policy based on national quotas necessarily implies discrimination, based upon some form of connection between the member state concerned and the ship, to decide who and who may not obtain the benefit of fishing against a national quota. Council Regulation 170/83, implementing the Common Fisheries Policy, uses the criterion of the flag of registration of the fishing vessel to decide which national quota its catch shall count against.

From about 1980 onwards, increasing numbers of Spanish vessels were re-registered as British vessels under the Merchant Shipping Act 1894, which was very permissive as to the effective nationality of the owners of vessels which could be registered as British. This practice was known as "quota hopping", since it permitted the re-registered Spanish vessels now to fish against the UK fisheries quota to the detriment of the British fishing industry. The Ministry of Agriculture became concerned at this practice, and made an initial attempt to curb it through fisheries licence conditions, but this proved ineffective.[30]

In 1988 the UK Parliament passed a new Merchant Shipping Act. It was framed to deal with the problem of "quota hopping". It restricted registration of fishing vessels under the British flag to ships owned or controlled by British individuals or British owned companies. The mere registration of a company in Britain was no longer sufficient.

Factortame and the other Spanish owned companies challenged the validity of the 1988 Act and the rules made under it. The challenge was important in itself, but gave rise to an even more important and wide-ranging constitutional question as to the status of an Act of Parliament before the courts of the United Kingdom if it is alleged not to conform to Community Law. The question of what happens if an Act is found, in a final decision, to be in conflict with Community law, has been considered at previously in this paper: but what happens on an interim basis when the courts have not yet ultimately decided on the validity of an Act?

The Queen's Bench Divisional Court held that in such circumstances it had the power to disapply an Act of Parliament on an interim basis pending final judgment;[31] the Court of Appeal reversed that decision, holding that under the United Kingdom constitution the courts have no power to disapply or suspend Acts of Parliament.[32] The House of Lords initially agreed with the Court of Appeal.[33]

In doing so, the House of Lords made reference to the legislative or quasi-legislative nature of such an act of interim suspension, if the power to do so were to exist in the court:[34]

"But an order granting the applicants the interim relief which they seek will only serve their purpose if it declares that which Parliament has enacted to be the law ... not to be the law until some uncertain future date ... If the applicants fail to establish the rights they claim before the ECJ, the effect of the interim relief granted would be to have conferred upon them rights directly contrary to Parliament's sovereign will and correspondingly to have deprived British fishing vessels, as defined by Parliament, of the enjoyment of a substantial proportion of the United Kingdom quota of stocks of fish protected by the Common Fisheries Policy. I am clearly of opinion that, as a matter of English law, the court has no power to make an order which has these consequences."

The House of Lords, however, referred the question of whether Community law required that the Courts should have interim power to suspend Acts of Parliament to the European Court, who ruled that:[35]

"a national court which, in a case before it concerning Community law, considers that the sole obstacle which precludes it from granting interim relief is a rule of national law must set aside that rule."

The House of Lords, in the light of the European Court's decision, granted interim relief effectively suspending the 1988 Act.[36] The upshot of this sequence of decisions calls for some comment from a jurisprudential point of view. The European Court dealt with the matter in negative terms as if there was a "rule" of English law which **prevented** a court from granting interim relief suspending an Act of Parliament, and once that "rule" was set aside or extinguished as incompatible with Community law then the English Court could exercise that power. But in truth there is no "rule" **against** the exercise by the English courts of such an interim power; it is just that no constitutional authority, whether by statute or under the common law, has conferred upon any court a power of such a nature, nor clothed the judges of any court with the authority to exercise it.

The creation of such a power, through the negative route of overriding a rule against its exercise, gives rise to a number of questions. Do all courts have this power, down to the lowest? Can a magistrates' court suspend an Act of Parliament, or is this function limited to the judges of the higher courts?

The new power is indeed wholly different from that of merely withholding or granting relief to the parties in a case. It is a substantive power to alter law, albeit on a temporary basis, which savours of being a legislative rather than a judicial act. It is not something which the courts have hitherto been used to undertaking under our constitution.

The *Factortame* case reached its final conclusion with the decision of the European Court[37] on the substantive question of the compatibility of the nationality rules of the 1988 Act with Community law. The Court ruled that they were not compatible with Article 52 of the Treaty of Rome, which provides for the freedom of establishment of individuals in other member states.

On the substantive issue, the overall conclusion of the case can only give rise to concern as to the basic fairness of what has occurred. Having agreed with its Community partners on a system of fishing quotas which would supposedly give fair protection to its fishing industry, the United Kingdom has then found itself in the position that other Treaty provisions have been successfully used to circumvent and to undermine that protection. It would be right to say that the effect of the ECJ's interpretation of the Treaty provisions has been that a different bargain has been delivered from that entered into.

The broader issues thrown up by the case relating to the powers of the Courts and the position of Acts of Parliament are of even greater importance. Are courts the right bodies to exercise a power to suspend Acts whose validity is contested? Does our constitution and history fit them to perform this role? How far does this power extend: in the ultimate, could the Courts even suspend or "disapply" an Act repealing or modifying the European Communities Act 1972?

3.3 Sunday Trading and Europe

The practice of the opening of shops at weekends varies widely across Europe. And why shouldn't it? National cultural conditions and social customs vary, and those may express themselves in widely different patterns of life at the weekend and on Sunday in particular. Furthermore, it is hard to think of an area of life which is less likely to have any impact on the other members states.

Sunday trading laws in England have been criticised as being anomalous and too restrictive. Indeed that is a criticism which I personally would share. However, Parliament last expressed a view when the liberalising Sunday Trading Bill was rejected by the House of Commons; and this essentially British social matter is surely a matter for the British to resolve through our own institutions.

It is therefore a matter of considerable surprise that the liberalisation of Sunday trading laws in England should be thought to be a matter of concern to Community law or Community institutions; but the effect of a series of legal decisions is that, surprisingly, this would appear to be the case.

In *Stoke-on-Trent City Council v. B & Q PLC*,[38] section 47 of the Shops Act 1957 was challenged on the grounds of its alleged incompatibility with Community law. The Shops Act was said to be contrary to Article 30 of the Treaty of Rome which prohibits "quantitative restrictions or measures having similar effect" on trade between member states. Initially drafted to outlaw explicit or disguised quotas on interstate trade, Article 30 has been successively interpreted in an expansive way through a series of judgments of the European Court. In *Dassonville*,[39] the ECJ stated as being within Article 30:

"All trading rules enacted by member states which are capable of hindering, directly or indirectly, actually or potentially, intra-Community trade are to be considered as measures having an effect equivalent to quantitative restrictions."

In the famous *Cassis de Dijon case*,[40] the ECJ made it clear that for the *Dassonville* test to apply, there did not have to be any difference in the application of the restriction concerned to imported and domestic goods. However, the restriction, although within Article 30, might then be permissible under Community law if it was justified to satisfy "mandatory requirements" relating to public health, the protection of the consumer or other matters.

Even on this more extended definition, it is hard to see how Sunday trading has any relationship to interstate trade. A nation accustomed to not buying its goods on Sundays will presumably go out and buy them instead on Saturdays or during the week. It is hard to see how this will place imported goods under any particular disadvantage as compared with domestic.

However, the European Court has ruled[41] that Sunday trading laws would be contrary to Article 30 of the Treaty of Rome unless "the restrictive effects on Community trade which may result therefrom do not exceed the effects intrinsic to rules of that kind." Whether or not this was so was "a question of fact to be determined by the national court."[42]

This part of the question having effectively been thrown back to the national courts by the ECJ, it was answered by Hoffmann J., in the *Stoke on Trent* case.[43] He held that the Sunday trading restrictions satisfied the test laid down by the ECJ, and so were not contrary to Community law. This decision has recently been approved by the ECJ,[44] but on a basis which calls for further analysis.

The approach to interpretation adopted by the European Court is of far wider interest than just in relation to this specific subject. Even though the Sunday trading laws of England have been held not to contravene Community law, this is on the ground that they are "justified" to achieve their objectives, and in the European Court's view comply with the Community law principle of "proportionality", i.e. that the means are proportional to the objectives pursued. The Court has not held that such measures are outside the scope of review by Community law because they do not affect interstate trade: quite the reverse.

By stretching the Treaty definition of "quantitative restrictions", the European Court has made Sunday trading laws, and all other laws which may have an effect on trade, even if there is no discrimination against imported goods, subject to the satisfaction of a battery of Community law tests, including the test of "proportionality". Thus, the ambit of the jurisdiction of Community law over national life has been effectively extended, with national laws being permitted to regulate only such residue of national affairs as Community law deems appropriate, subject to its rules of proportionality and justification.

Even this residue is granted to the Member States somewhat grudgingly:

"National rules governing the opening hours of retail premises reflect certain political and economic choices in so far as their purpose is to ensure that working hours are arranged so as to accord with national or regional socio-cultural characteristics, and that, in the present state of Community law, is a matter for Member States."[45]

The reference to "the present state of Community law", which appears frequently in judgments of the Court, indicates that the Court envisages the day when member states will no longer have such a residue of discretion permitted to them.

If an area so far remote from inter-state trade as Sunday trading laws has been brought under the umbrella of a "quantitative restriction" in this way, there must be many other areas of national life which would, unexpectedly, also be subject to that jurisdiction and therefore to Community law tests of "justification" and of "proportionality".

The attitude of the European Court to the interpretation of Article 30 does indeed pose considerable questions, dealt with in more detail in Chapter 5.6 below, as to the attitude which the Court will adopt in interpreting Article 100a of the Treaty which permits the introduction of "Single Market" measures by a majority voting procedure, so potentially providing a route to circumvent the unanimous vote required for "Social Charter" issues.

A final aspect of this topic is potentially a cause for some amusement. It now seems quite possible that the adoption, against the United Kingdom's wishes, of the 48-hour working week directive now under discussion could defeat the objectives of the Sunday trading lobby, and render Sunday trading more restricted than under the present UK laws. Thus, those who seek to live by the European sword may well end up dying by it; and at a point in time when it seems quite likely that at long last there will be a renewed Parliamentary effort to bring some measure of liberalising reform to the laws of Sunday trading.

However, whatever the amusement value of such an outcome, it would in fact be a sad development. It would represent the loss of the United Kingdom Parliament's power to regulate in accordance with our democratic wishes an aspect of purely internal social policy. No wider Community good would thereby be served; no benefit would accrue through a better or more efficient common market. Such an outcome would merely have seen prevail a wholly irrational approach to the scope of Community law and the powers of Community institutions, and seen the triumph of uniform European regulation and harmonisation for its own sake without regard to whether any European interest is thereby served and without regard to the cultural and social individuality of the Member States.

Sunday trading may not, by itself, be a very important aspect of the social life of this country. But if this is the approach applied to Sunday trading, then what other aspects of social life, however remote they may seem from questions of inter-state trade, will next be subject to the application of Community law?

3.4 Border Controls and the Internal Market

The Single European Act inserted into the Treaty of Rome a new article, Art 8a, which provides for the establishment of the "internal market" by 1st January 1993. It says:

"The internal market shall comprise an area without frontiers in which the free movement of goods, persons, services and capital is ensured in accordance with the provisions of the this Treaty."

On the face of it, this provision would appear to require that both customs points and passport controls should be abolished as from 1st January 1993. The policy of the British Government is however firmly against the removal of such controls at points of entry to the United Kingdom. Accordingly, a "declaration" was negotiated at the time of the Single European Act which reads:

"Nothing in these provisions shall affect the right of Member States to take such measures as they consider necessary for the purpose of controlling immigration from third countries, and to combat terrorism, crime, the traffic in drugs and illicit trading in works of art and antiques."

The British Government maintains that this declaration gives it the right to maintain passport and customs checks at its borders, but the Commission and others challenge this interpretation. Who is right, the British Government or the Commission?

It was announced last year that the British Government had reached an informal agreement with Mr Martin Bangemann, the Commissioner responsible for the internal market, under which the Commission would not take action against the continuation of limited passport checks which involve waving the outside cover of a European Community passport at an immigration officer. This is known as "the Bangemann wave". Unfortunately for the British Government, this deal with the Commission is of little value since Article 8a is part of directly applicable Community law and any private individual can challenge the legality of these controls through the British courts, who will then be obliged to refer the matter to the ECJ under Article 177.

A German Euro-MP and at least one Brussels based group have announced their intentions to make such legal challenges early in 1993. The question is therefore not whether, but when, the British Government's position will be considered by the European Court.

The British Government may be right in thinking that it secured a declaration which it and other member states regarded at the time as reserving a right to maintain border controls for those purposes. However, the wording is hardly explicit, and the reference in Article 8a to an area "without frontiers" does not sit happily with the right to maintain general checks which is argued for by the British Government. In addition, a "declaration" is of less legal strength than a Treaty provision. It is of persuasive rather than substantive legal force.

Furthermore, the question will be answered not by an impartial and dispassionate interpreter of the provisions of the Treaty, but by the European Court of Justice, a committed Community institution whose jurisprudence is considered in more detail in Chapter 4.2 below. There cannot, therefore, be room for any great confidence that the British Government's views on this question will ultimately prevail.

What will be the effect of the Maastricht Treaty on this question? It has been reported[46] that "sources close to the Foreign Secretary" have indicated that Britain's chances of winning such a court case would be strengthened by the clause in the Maastricht Treaty which will introduce the principle of "subsidiarity" into the Treaty of Rome. The Foreign Office booklet, "Britain in Europe", claims that nothing in the Maastricht Treaty alters the position on frontier controls.[47]

On this question, the Foreign Office appears either to be proceeding on poor advice or to be gratuitously misleading. The Maastricht clause on "subsidiarity" is considered in more detail in Chapter 5.2 below, but it plainly is of no assistance in this dispute if only because it applies to subordinate measures, not to directly applicable Treaty provisions such as Article 8a. Nor does it modify Treaty objectives themselves, or apply to areas falling within the Community's "exclusive competence" such as the internal market.

On the other hand, there are other important aspects of the Maastricht Treaty which would strengthen rather than weaken the case that the maintenance of border controls is contrary to the creation of the "European Union" which is envisaged. Article 8a(1) confers on every Union citizen the express right to move freely within the Community. Most significantly, new Article 100c establishes a common Community system for granting visas to nationals of non-Community countries, implying that non-Community nationals are to be checked at the point of entry to the Community, so that checking at intra-Community borders is no longer justified.

Chapter 4

Principles of Development of the EEC

4.1 Can Sovereignty be "Pooled"?

"The transfer by the States from their domestic legal system to the Community legal system of the rights and obligations arising under the Treaty carries with it a permanent limitation of their sovereign rights, against which a subsequent unilateral act incompatible with the concept of the Community cannot prevail;"

The European Court of Justice in *Costa v. ENEL*.[48]

The European Court of Justice's above statement as to the effect of Community law on the sovereignty of Member States is the Court's most well known pronouncement on the subject of sovereignty. The Court in a later case[49] restated the proposition in stronger terms: "The Member States' assignment of rights and powers to the Community in accordance with the provisions of the Treaty entails a definitive limitation of their sovereign rights against which no provisions of municipal law, whatever their nature, can be legally invoked." It should be noted that "municipal" law is lawyers' terminology for the law of a sovereign state, as opposed to international law: it has nothing to do with local government.

The concept of sovereignty, and of the surrender of sovereignty, has given rise to much debate. The word has a range of different meanings. Strictly, it is the ultimate authority of a State to legislate. In federal states, such as Germany and the USA, aspects of this authority may be delegated downwards to subordinate units, but sovereignty resides at the federal level because the federal constitution governs what powers are allowed to the subordinate units. Legislative authority in some spheres may be delegated upwards by sovereign States to international bodies, such as NATO. However the ultimate authority, and therefore sovereignty, still resides with the member States because they decide the scope of powers which NATO may exercise and ultimately may withdraw from NATO so ending its delegated authority to exercise powers on their behalf.[50]

The EEC is probably still in the category where sovereignty in this strict sense resides with the Member States, and the Community has a delegated, rather than sovereign, authority to legislate in fields laid down by the Treaties. This is because the Member States still have the ultimate power to determine the boundaries of the Community's Treaty powers (even though these boundaries may be extended by generous "interpretation" by the European Court of Justice) and, at least as part of their own internal laws, have a theoretical legal power to disapply Community law if they were to choose to do so.[51]

The present course of development of the Community does not have to proceed much further, however, before these propositions will cease to be so, and sovereignty in its strict sense will reside with the Community. The Member States will then have delegated to them the exercise of such legislative authority as the Community shall allow, with the Community being the ultimate arbiter of the scope of those powers. The doctrine of "subsidiarity", discussed in more detail in section 5.2 below, dangerously evokes that concept.

The word "sovereignty" is however quite widely used, and some would say misused,[52] to mean merely effective power or control, rather than legal authority. Used in this looser sense, it can be argued that no nation is unaffected by events outside its borders.

So, it is argued, by making over aspects of our affairs to common European institutions, we share in the formulation of the policy which governs those aspects. In many instances, those aspects of our affairs are in any event so far affected by world or external influences that we have little effective "sovereignty" over them, so that by "pooling" our sovereignty, we are effectively increasing it.

Even accepting this as a legitimate use of the word "sovereignty", rather than a confusion of concepts designed to obscure a real question, the substance of this argument requires examination. Can the "pooling" of decision-making over aspects of our affairs into common European institutions, in whose joint policies we have our say, lead to greater effective control for us over those aspects of our affairs?

It seems obvious that there are instances where this will be the case, but defining the extent of the circumstances where this may be so calls for further consideration. It may be useful first to consider circumstances where "pooling" will **not** lead to any increase in effective control.

(1) **Essentially internal matters:** The concept of increasing sovereignty by "pooling" it can have no validity in instances where the matters affected are purely internal matters over which, in the absence of common European regulation, we in any event have complete autonomy. The example is given above of Sunday trading. Transferring the power to regulate Sunday trading to Brussels necessarily dimishes the degree of freedom of action (or "sovereignty" even in this looser sense) enjoyed by the British people and Parliament, since we are no longer free to regulate this aspect of our national life in accordance with our own wishes expressed through our democratic processes. It is of no value or interest to the British people that we thereby obtain, through the Community institutions, a power to influence and regulate Sunday trading hours in, say, Italy.

It is plain that many other aspects of what the EEC currently regulates, or seeks the powers to regulate, wholly fail to satisfy this test. The effect of European regulation of these matters must therefore be a net loss, not an increase through "pooling", of the sovereignty of member states.

(2) **Basic concordance of interests:** If the matters concerned can perfectly well be left to the individual decisions of the Member States, so that different states may pursue different policies without seriously impinging on each other, then there can be no conceivable advantage in "pooling" sovereignty over those matters. However, even if it is a matter on which there might be advantages in having a common policy, there is a second, and very important, fundamental condition for "pooling" to lead to an effective increase of our sovereignty. Those with whom we pool the sovereignty must have interests which are basically similar to our own.

If they do not, then instead of being able to exert such influence as we may as an independent nation in order to forward our interests, we are shackled into a system where we are unable to forward our own interests but on the contrary must subordinate them to contrary interests dictated by the majority vote of others.

Perhaps the most important field of EEC affairs where this basic incompatibility of interest applies is that of agriculture. The fundamental differences between the structure of agriculture in the United Kingdom and that in the major Continental countries, France, Germany and Italy, makes this field a constant source of potential subjugation of the British national interest to the contrary interests of other Member States. Until recently, we have seen the current Uruguay round of the GATT negotiations, where we have to negotiate as part of the EEC as a bloc, stalled for years. Our interests, as a manufacturing and trading nation, in free trade on a worldwide scale have been subordinated to the insistence of the EEC on maintaining agricultural subsidies at a level far higher than we as a nation would independently wish them to be.

The Common Agricultural Policy reforms agreed upon by the Council of Ministers in May 1992 are supposed to alleviate the problem of agricultural over-production and export dumping, and so, it is hoped, remove the blockage in GATT. The December 1992 agreement in principle between the Commission and the United States may, it is hoped, now allow progress towards conclusion of the Uruguay round. However, France's determined rearguard action in defence of its farming interests is likely to be bought off, if at all, by expensive concessions on top of those already given under the terms of the CAP reforms. These involve a highly expensive and apparently permanent system of agricultural subsidies, coupled with a massively bureaucratic system of production controls at the level of individual farms.

Thus, on the important matter of agriculture we see the fundamental differences in national interest between ourselves and other member states causing a situation in which only constant conflict and struggle prevents British agricultural and wider trading interests being sacrificed for the sake of the uneconomic small-farm based agricultures of other member states. Where British farmers are not sacrificed it only seems to be at the expense of British tax payers. It is difficult in the field of agriculture to say that our sovereignty has been effectively increased by "pooling".

It is possible to argue that this disadvantage is counterbalanced by other advantages of EEC membership, and in particular the advantages of free trade within the non-agricultural common market. Indeed, at the time of Britain's entry in 1972, acceptance of the Common Agricultural Policy was widely presented as Britain's "entry ticket" in return for which we would receive the benefits to industry of joining the common market. That, however, is not saying that our sovereignty in the field of agriculture is effectively increased by pooling it; on the contrary, it is accepting that it is reduced but saying that other benefits compensate for that reduction.

A further, clear, example of where divergence of interests would lead to a loss of effective sovereignty, were it to be pooled or merged, can be seen in the field of foreign policy in the context of the Gulf war. The reluctance of the majority of our European partners to take any action was widely perceived to be contrary to our national interest. We were able however as an independent nation to pursue our own course of successful action in that war. Had our sovereignty in that respect been pooled or merged, we would not have been able to do so.

This discussion does show that the concept of increasing "sovereignty" (used in the looser sense of power or control rather than legal sovereignty) through pooling can have validity. However, the circumstances under which this is so are circumscribed by the two fundamental conditions discussed above: (1) that we are regulating a matter which is not best left in any event to diverse national solutions; and (2) that there is a basic congruity of interests in the matter concerned with those with whom we "pool" sovereignty.

4.2 The role of the European Court of Justice

The European Court of Justice has a central role in the interpretation of Community law, and in its application to and within member states.[53] In one sense its role is subordinate to those of the political institutions of the Community and the Member States, since they between them have devised the Treaty provisions which have created the Court and which the Court interprets; and the subordinate legislation which also the Court must interpret.

In another sense, however, the Court's role is superior to those of the political institutions and Member States, since it can, through the interpretation which it gives to the Treaties and other Community laws, fundamentally affect the balance between the Community institutions and the Member States. In its role it is unhindered by the procedural requirements (e.g. unanimous or qualified majority votes in the Council of Ministers) which apply to the political processes which explicitly make amendments to Community law. It is therefore important to ask whether the Court is an impartial referee and interpreter of the Treaty provisions and rules made by the Member States and the political institutions of the Community, or whether it fulfils its interpretative task in a different way.

The Court is based in Luxembourg. It consists of 13 judges[54] whose appointments are effectively shared out by Member States. These judges are not, however, in any sense representatives of the member states who appoint them and, like members of the Commission, their oaths of office expressly forbid them to act for or on behalf of any Member State.

The judges take up permanent residence in Luxembourg for their term of office of 6 years[55] (which may be renewed). It is not surprising that those drawn to membership of the Court are necessarily judges to whom the European ideal has appeal, nor that, in their collegiate atmosphere there, the judges of the court come to see themselves as an integral part of the process of promoting European unity. In no sense can the Court be regarded as a neutral arbitral body, impartially holding the balance between the central European institutions and the Member States. It is avowedly part of those central European institutions, partisan in favour of promoting their powers and duties at the expense of those of Member States where they conflict with what the Court sees as the overall thrust of the Treaties. A very early indication of the attitude of the Court can be seen in *Netherlands v. High Authority*,[56] where the power of the Court to rule on complaints against member states referred to it is described as:

" ... the ultima ratio enabling the Community interests enshrined in the Treaty to prevail over the inertia and resistance of Member States."

A further important matter to be appreciated is the practice of the Court with regard to judgments. Dissenting judgments are not allowed. Only a majority judgment is published, and it is not revealed which judges have voted in favour of it and which against; nor indeed whether or not there has been any dissent at all. This rule was designed to protect individual judges from undue pressure from the Member State which appointed them: for example it would be embarrassing if it were revealed that a judge had concurred in an important decision against his own country. It does however have the unwelcome side effect that judicial debate within the Court, if such occurs, does not see the light of day.

The Court has avowedly acted as an architect of European integration.[57]

Apart from an approach to jurisprudence which involves basing its judgments not so much on specific provisions as upon general principles or objectives of the Treaties, the ECJ has found a new and fruitful source of jurisprudence in applying "the general principles common to the laws of the Member States." However, in applying this source of jurisprudence the approach of the Court has been stated as "not simply to take a more or less arithmetical average of the different municipal solutions, but to choose those solutions from among the various legal systems prevailing in the different Member States as, having regard to the objectives of the Treaty, appeared to it the best, or if one may use the word, the most progressive."[58]

Upon the basis of this principle, the Court has applied principles in accordance with its view of "fundamental rights" of individuals, even though such rights have no explicit recognition in the Treaties.[59]

Examples of the Court's interpretative approach have been given above, in the case particularly of the issue of equal pay for women. Perhaps one further illustration will assist. This concerns the subject of direct applicability of directives.

As explained in Chapter 2.1 above, directives are envisaged by Article 189(3) of the Treaty as being binding on Member States but not (at least explicitly) as causing any direct effects under the laws of the

Member States. It is probable that the framers of the Treaties saw directives as being enforceable only on the plane of international law, i.e against Member States only under the mechanisms of Articles 169 and 170 of the Treaty at the suit of the Commission or other Member States.[60]

A series of decisions of the Court has, however, radically altered that position. In *Van Duyn v. Home Office*,[61] the ECJ held that directives could, if sufficiently clear, be relied upon directly by individuals in domestic courts in cases **against** Member States. Thus, although a directive would not directly alter the law of a Member State so as to allow, for example, one citizen to sue another, they did permit the citizen to sue the State itself.

The doctrine devised by the Court does give rise to some difficulties. Directives are to have direct effect under the laws of Member State but only in a specific context, actions against the State itself, which may have an arbitrary relationship to the provisions of the directive. For example, directives concerning conditions of employment cannot be directly enforced in actions against employers, unless the employer happens to be "the State". This gives rise to an arbitrary division of employees into two categories, those employed by "the State" and those employed by others, the former of whom can rely upon the directive and the latter of whom cannot.

This in turn gives rise to the question of what is the "State" for the purposes of being bound by a directive, even though this question is of no relevance to the terms of the directive itself which does not seek to distinguish between State and non-State employees. *Foster v. British Gas PLC*,[62] a case about Directive 76/207 on equality of employment provisions, produced the anomalous result that British Gas PLC, although now privatised, was bound by the directive as part of "the State" since it had been a nationalised industry at the time when events giving rise to the case occurred. This and other cases[63] have widened "the State" to a potentially large class of bodies.

The anomalous effect of that particular decision on the now private company does illustrate some of the logical and legal difficulty involved in the doctrine of direct effect of directives as created by the Court. The doctrine is, in the words of the Court, based upon the need as perceived by the Court to ensure the "effectiveness"[64] of Community measures rather than upon the actual terms of Article 189 of the Treaty of Rome (as quoted previously). The Court, in order to give vent to its frustration at what it sees as the backsliding or obstructiveness of Member States in implementing directives, would appear to have distorted the ordinary and plain meaning of the Treaty provisions in order to achieve its favoured objective, despite the logical absurdities involved.

More recently, the doctrine of direct effect of directives has been extended by the Court so that individuals may sue the State for damages in the national courts for breach of directives.

The role of the Court will be of even greater importance after the coming into force of the Treaty of Maastricht - it will have to interpret the Treaties to decide what measures may be introduced by majority vote and which require unanimity. It will have to decide what measures may be taken under the Social provisions of the existing Treaties, and what measures may only be taken under the new Agreement on Social Policy attached to the Maastricht Treaty, to which the United Kingdom is not a party.

The Court's history illustrates that it may not be expected to exercise this role impartially. This does raise the question, considered further in Chapter 5.6 below, of whether the British Government in excluding the Social chapter from the Maastricht Treaty has in fact achieved a substantial, or merely a hollow, victory. It will be for the Court through its interpretations of Treaty provisions to decide whether or not that exclusion may be effectively circumvented.

4.3 "Federalism" and the importance of general words

"On balance the emerging European Community fits, in the light of the EEC Treaty, better into a federal than confederal form... The Treaty is not a mere contractual compact, it is an institutional stage of European unity." Lasok and Bridge,
"Law and Institutions of the European Communities", 5th Edition.

Much publicity was given to the stance of the British Government in resisting the inclusion of the word "federal" in the Maastricht Treaty. How important would have been the inclusion in the Treaty of a reference to the European Community as a "federal" body, and what has been achieved by the omission of this specific description?

Under common law traditions of legal interpretation, we are used to a system where what is important are the specific words of relevant substantive provisions. General prefatory words are regarded merely as background against which the relevant provisions are interpreted.

Such a tradition seems to have underlain the British Government's attitude to the negotiation of Treaty changes, most notably those embodied in the Single European Act, and a number of Community directives and regulations. So long as the specific concrete provisions are acceptable, not too much attention has been focussed on flowery general introductory language.

However, it is a mistake to assume that such general language is unimportant, particularly bearing in mind that the Treaties and other texts embodying Community law will be interpreted in accordance with Continental, rather than common law, legal traditions.

It is worth looking at some of the more important pieces of general wording. The preamble to the Treaty of Rome declares that its signatories are "Determined to lay the foundations of an ever closer union among the peoples of Europe".

Article 5 of the Treaty provides that: "Member States shall take all appropriate measures, whether general or particular, to ensure fulfilment of the obligations arising out of this Treaty or resulting from the actions taken by the institutions of the Community. They shall facilitate the achievement of the Community's tasks. They shall abstain from any measure which could jeopardise the attainment of the objectives of this Treaty."

The objectives of the Treaty are interpreted in the light of the preamble. There are then generally expressed provisions requiring Member States to facilitate the attainment of those objectives. This provides ample material for both the Court and other Community institutions, if they are inclined to do so, to interpret those provisions as imposing quite extensive and mandatory duties upon Member States. It is dangerous agreeing to such terms upon the assumption that they can be treated as mere verbiage.

In the case of *Van Gend en Loos*, (as quoted previously), the European Court based its fundamental decision as to the nature of Community law, as "a new legal order" comprising not only Member States but their nationals, upon the preamble to the Treaty of Rome, and in particular its references "not only to governments but to peoples."[65]

The wording of the Rome Treaty preamble was also relied upon by the ECJ in the *Defrenne v. SABENA* case (referred to above in the discussion on equal pay), where the Court noted that the objective of the Community to ensure social progress and seek the constant improvement of the living and working conditions of their peoples was "emphasized by the Preamble to the Treaty."[66]

The general objectives of the Rome Treaty are carried further in the Single European Act of 1986. It is worth setting out much of the preamble to the Single European Act in full:

"Moved by the will to continue the work undertaken on the basis of the Treaties establishing the European Communities and to transform relations as a whole among their States into a European Union ..."

"Resolved to implement this European Union ... and to invest this union with the necessary means of action."

"Determined to work together to promote democracy on the basis of the fundamental rights recognised in the constitutions and laws of Member States, in the [European Human Rights Convention] and the European Social Charter ..."

"Determined to improve the economic and social situation by extending common policies and pursuing new objectives ..."

"Whereas ... the Heads of State or of Government approved the objective of the progressive realisation of Economic and Monetary Union ..."

And Article 1 of the Single European Act states that:

"The European Communities and European Political Co-operation shall have as their objective to contribute together to making concrete progress towards European unity."

All these general words cited above are of great importance, particularly having regard to the interpretative approach of the European Court. Its judgments make repeated references to interpreting Community law with reference to the objectives of the Treaties. And it is to be noted that all the references set out above are already part of the existing Treaties, without needing to refer to the further objectives set out in the Treaty of Maastricht.

Against this background it is surprising that the Prime Minister John Major should have stated that the Preamble to the Maastricht Treaty is just "Euro-waffle" which has "no legal force whatsoever."[67] Both *Van Gend en Loos* and *Defrenne* are landmark decisions of the European Court, and that Court's so-called "teleological" approach to interpretation is contrasted with the traditional English common law approach in the most basic courses for law students on Community law. It is disturbing in the extreme that the advice given to the Prime Minister should apparently contain so basic a misconception.

There have been occasions in the past when a British Government has congratulated itself on a victory when it has secured the watering down of unwelcome substantive provisions at the expense of agreeing to "mere windy generalities" in the text concerned. This, however, in the long term may not be a victory at all, as the text can be interpreted in the light of those windy generalities to have a meaning wholly different from what might be envisaged from the substantive provisions taken by themselves. I will consider this aspect of the Maastricht Treaty more extensively in the next Chapter.

Chapter 5

The Treaty of Maastricht

5.1 Outline of the Treaty

The formal title of the Treaty of Maastricht is the "Treaty on European Union". It is the outcome of two intergovernmental conferences, on economic and monetary union and political union respectively, and of a stormy European summit meeting held at Maastricht in December 1991.

It contains new provisions of its own, and extensively amends the Treaty of Rome. In the last Chapter, I considered the effect of general wordings and preambles in the subsequent interpretation of Community instruments. It is therefore worth setting out some of the more fundamental general provisions of the Maastricht Treaty.

By Article A, the parties "establish amongst themselves a European Union, hereafter called 'the Union' ". By the preamble, the parties are "resolved to establish as citizenship common to nationals of their countries", and Article G(C) establishes "Citizenship of the Union" which it confers on every person holding the nationality of a Member State.

Article G(A) alters the name of the "European Economic Community" established by the Treaty of Rome to the "European Community", so removing any remaining presumption which was derived from its name that its purposes are only or mainly economic. Article G(B) alters the objectives of the Community by amending Article 2 of the Treaty of Rome as follows (inserted words emboldened):

"The Community shall have as its task, by establishing a common market and an economic and monetary union and by implementing the common policies or activities referred to in Articles 3 and 3a, to promote throughout the Community a harmonious and balanced development of economic activities, sustainable and non-inflationary growth respecting the environment, a high degree of convergence of economic performance,

a high level of employment and of social protection, the raising of the standard of living and quality of life, and economic and social cohesion and solidarity among Member States. "

The Treaty establishes a new European Central Bank and provides for the establishment of a single currency in three stages. Member States are required to "regard their economic policies as a matter of common concern" and to obey "broad guidelines of the economic policies of the member states" formulated by the Council of Ministers.[68] In order to ensure compliance with the guidelines, a system of "multilateral surveillance" is established[69] and the Council may make "recommendations" to Member States whose policies are "not consistent" with the guidelines.[70]

Member States are required to avoid "excessive government deficits",[71] and non-compliance with this provision may result in a procedure ending with the imposition of fines or other sanctions on the Member State concerned.[72] Extensive powers over monetary policy are to be conferred upon the new independent European Central Bank. Member States are required during the second stage of monetary union to start the process of making their own central banks independent.[73]

The process of transition to the 3rd stage of monetary union is stated by a Protocol to the Treaty to be of "irreversible character". Another Protocol however gives the United Kingdom the right to opt-out of the third stage of monetary union, although not the first or second stages.

Clearly, the economic and monetary union provisions do involve a fundamental transfer of important aspects of national sovereignty to the Community institutions. These are significant in the first and second stages, and even more profound in the third stage of monetary union.

Apart from its provisions on monetary union, the Treaty contains wide ranging provisions on a common European foreign policy envisaged to lead ultimately to a common European defence policy, social policy, education and training, culture, public health, consumer protection, trans-European transport networks, a European Development Fund to make transfer payments from richer to poorer areas, and industry and research and technical development. The powers of the Community over the environment are extensively widened.

The common European foreign policy provisions are in a separate section of the Maastricht Treaty, outside the amendments to the Treaty of Rome. This is said, particularly by the British Government, to make this policy "intergovernmental" and to limit the extent of involvement by the Community institutions. I shall examine this claim in more depth in section 5.3 below.

The powers of the European Parliament in the Community legislative process are extended. In one provision of particular political importance within the United Kingdom, the European Parliament is given a veto right over the proposals which it is to draw up for a uniform electoral procedure (for elections to itself) in all Member States. These proposals will almost inevitably be based on proportional representation.[74]

All in all, leaving aside the foreign and defence policy aspects, the Treaty of Maastricht involves a considerable further extension of the already wide areas of policy matters internal to Member States to which Community law is capable of being applied. The potential certainly exists, if the Community institutions wish to follow this course, for very much more extensive secondary legislation (regulations and directives) extending into and regulating all the areas of national life listed above.

It is therefore of crucial importance the extent to which the Community institutions will in fact make use of the opportunities given to them under the Treaty to legislate in all these areas. The British Government has set much store by its achievement in enshrining the principle of "subsidiarity" into the Maastricht Treaty. It is therefore worth next considering the extent to which this is likely to lead to a change in the behaviour pattern which the Community institutions have exhibited in the past.

5.2 "Subsidiarity" in theory and in practice

"Subsidiarity" is a word which is meaningless to most people. It has, however, recently become a vogue word amongst those dealing with the European Communities. It describes, or is supposed to describe, the concept that any decision should be taken at the lowest possible level: for example, decisions which do not bear on or affect other member states should be taken at national level or below.

The principle is to be formally adopted as part of Community law as part of the Maastricht Treaty, which defines subsidiarity in a new Article 3b, to be inserted into the Treaty of Rome, as follows:

"In areas which do not fall within its exclusive competence, the Community shall take action, in accordance with the principle of subsidiarity, only if and in so far as the objectives of the proposed action cannot be sufficiently achieved by the Member States and can, therefore, by reason of the scale or effects of the proposed action, be better achieved by the Community. "

It is suggested that by application of this principle, decisions and activities of the Community institutions will be kept within bounds and powers restored to national levels where they belong.

First, the doctrine of subsidiarity itself. It is of Papal origin,[75] and advocates the desirability of devolving power down to the lowest possible level. The very idea, however, involves the inevitability that it will be the centre which decides what power it thinks appropriate to devolve to the lower levels of the hierarchy.

The very concept intrinsically lacks a further vital element, namely democratic consent from the Member States to decisions of any particular kind being decided at European level, irrespective of whether it may be the view of the central European institutions that they ought to be decided at that level. It carries the danger that there will be a presumption that all decisions of importance should take place at the European level, with only a residue of decisions relegated to national level, as crumbs from the table of the Community institutions.

Next, it is worth examining the wording of the definition of subsidiarity in new clause 3b quite carefully.[76] The first point is that it is not stated to be relevant to the interpretation of directly applicable Treaty provisions themselves: it concerns action taken by the Community **under** the Treaties, such as regulations and directives. More importantly, it applies only to areas which "do not fall within [the Community's] exclusive competence". This, in accordance with the "occupied field" doctrine,[77] rules out its application to vast areas of Community law.

Its application is therefore limited to areas where the Treaties provide for competence both on the part of the Community and on the part of the Member States. In those fields, Community action is permitted where the "objectives of the proposed action" can "by reason of the scale or effects of the proposed action, be better achieved by the Community."

It is important to note that this clause in no way requires that matters internal to a Member State and which do not affect any other Member State should be left to be dealt with by the Member State. It merely refers to the "objectives of the proposed action" as the justification for action at Community level. To give an example, it is an objective of the Community that there should be "a high level of social protection".[78] The Community is therefore entitled, under the terms of new article 3b, to take action to impose on Member States requirements to provide a certain level of "social protection" since this is an objective of the Treaty and the objective of the proposed measures. Since the objective is itself internal to Member States, it does not matter for the purposes of Article 3b if such measures would have no effect whatsoever on other member states or upon the functioning of the internal market.

The Article 3b definition of subsidiarity simply asks whether Community or national action will be better at attaining Community-defined objectives. This is in fact a very limited definition of subsidiarity which falls a long way short of what subsidiarity is understood to mean according to most political expectations. This is subsidiarity only in the mode of achievement of a programme of objectives laid down by the Community. As such, it reserves for Member States the role of agents for the implementation of Community policies, in cases where the Community sees fit to allow them to carry out this role.

Even within the very narrow and restricted scope of the test of "subsidiarity" as set out in Article 3b, its form makes it almost impossible for a Court to apply it in practice so as to strike down a Community measure as contravening it. Lord Mackenzie Stuart, former President of the European Court, has condemned the definition as "gobbledygook", and considers that it renders a court's task in applying it almost impossible because questions about the relative "effectiveness" of Community or national action are likely to be incapable of judicial resolution.[79] Courts will confine themselves merely to asking whether the legislative body (Commission or Council of Ministers) has gone through the motions of considering the question of subsidiarity. Routine paragraphs will be inserted claiming that subsidiarity has been considered by the Council or Commission, and these will almost always be sufficient to fend off a legal challenge.

The manifest deficiencies of Article 3b of the Maastricht Treaty led the British Government to seek to clarify or strengthen the principle of subsidiarity, but without seeking to amend the defective Treaty text itself. These efforts culminated in two interpretative "declarations" at the Birmingham summit meeting on 16 October 1992 and at the Edinburgh summit on 11-12 December 1992. What have these done to remedy the deficiencies of the Treaty text itself?

Regrettably, very little, and in some respects the guidelines adopted have emphasised or exacerbated those deficiencies. What would have been of use would have been guidelines relating to specific policy areas, such as social policy, competition, etc. The guidelines adopted are purely general. The Edinburgh declaration states that the principle of subsidiarity "does not relate to and cannot call into question the powers conferred on the European Community by the Treaty as interpreted by the Court ... The application of the principle shall respect the general principle and shall respect the general provisions of the Maastricht Treaty, including the 'maintaining in full of the acquis communautaire', and it shall not affect the primacy of Community law." Maintenance of the "acquis communautaire" implies the preservation under Community control of the powers the Community has already acquired.

Paragraph (ii) of the guidelines make it clear that there is no need at all for a measure to have "transnational aspects" in order for it to satisfy Article 3b: it is quite sufficient that it should be directed to the attainment of a Treaty objective (which may be purely internal to member states) such as that of "strengthening economic and social cohesion".

The emphasis of the guidelines is on adopting "lighter forms" of Community legislation, e.g. directives instead of regulations and leaving more discretion to Member States in working out the details. This re-emphasises the true scope of subsidiarity as embodied in the Maastricht Treaty: reserving an agency role for Member States in implementing Community policies.

The next question to ask is to what extent the general principle set out in Article 3b will be effective in practice? That question can best be answered by asking to what extent the activities of the Community institutions to date have revealed regard for the independence of the Member States.

The clear answer is that the behaviour of Community institutions to date – and in particular that of the Commission – does not give any reason to suppose that this principle will, in the absence of profound institutional change, have much if any actual effect upon the behaviour and aspirations of those institutions nor on the onward march of European "harmonisation" for harmonisation's sake.

Considered simply as a legal barrier, the new Article 3b is likely to be of limited effectiveness. There will always be arguments, however tenuous, that the "scale" or "effects" of any proposed action justify legislation at Community level. For an example, see the instance of Sunday trading laws discussed above: it is said that if shops do not open on Sunday, then it may by some means or other have an effect on goods imported from other Member States, and this was used as a justification for bringing the ambit of Sunday trading laws within the scope of Community jurisdiction.

Similarly, many, if not all, aspects of the Social Charter may be justified on the grounds that they have a potential effect upon the competitiveness of businesses, and therefore potentially affect competition within the single market. If employees in one member state are restricted to working 48 hours a week, and employees in another are not so restricted, will the latter not have a competitive advantage? Does not this supply a ground, applying the doctrine of subsidiarity, why a decision on this matter should be taken at European rather than at national level?

These examples illustrate that if the institutions which are given by the Treaties the task of interpreting this provision are committed to a particular view of what should be regulated by Brussels, "subsidiarity" will not stand in their way.

It therefore becomes vital to examine closely the make up and behaviour of the institutions concerned to see the extent to which they are likely to observe the principle in practice.

What are the institutions? The most important for practical purposes is the Commission. This now consists of 17 members elected by the national governments. In theory, the whole Commission is elected by all the national governments acting together, but in practice each country nominates either one or two individual Commissioners, depending on its size. Each Commissioner has to be given a portfolio. The portfolios include Agriculture, Environment, Industrial Affairs and Technology, Employment and Social Affairs, Science and Education, Agriculture, Competition, Economy, Culture, Budget, Immigration and Home Affairs, External Affairs and lastly, but by no means least, the President of the Commission.

Each Commissioner has a vested interest in making his or her portfolio as important as possible; the President of the Commission, M. Delors, has a vested interest in making the role of the Commission and its President as important as possible.

Many of the Commission portfolios are inherently unrelated to either the single market or to any other matters on which it can be said that there is genuinely any need for pan-European regulation. Thus the very existence of these portfolios, staffed by power hungry politicians with empire-building civil servants underneath them, is a challenge to the principle of subsidiarity.

The next body to consider in this context is the European Parliament. Is this body likely to provide any barrier to the spread of European control or to assist in the maintenance of the principle of subsidiarity in the Community?

The answer is no. Members of the European Parliament are attracted to become candidates for membership of that body largely because of their "pro-European" outlook. To some of them, there are positive attractions in building up the power of the central European institutions in order to increase their own power: Mrs Edwina Currie MP is reported as saying that she wishes to stand for election to the European Parliament because she wants a position in "the youngest, biggest superpower in the world. Being in the right place at the right time in Europe, a person can achieve a lot."[80] Collectively, the Parliament behaves in an even more integrationist way than its members do individually.

If the Parliament cannot be relied upon to assist in maintaining a fair balance between the European central institutions and the Member States, then what about the Court? It is the Court after all which is charged with the task of interpreting the Treaties and other instruments which embody Community law and, therefore, ultimately the task of properly delimiting the scope of the Treaties.

Chapter 4.2 above has extensively considered the history of the Court's role. It is not, and is not suited to be, a body which impartially interprets the proper bounds of the Community's role in the affairs of Member States.

The conclusions of this Section are clear and can be shortly stated:

(1) The doctrine of "subsidiarity" is so vague that it will not by itself provide any effective limitation upon the ambit of Community action.

(2) The drafting of Article 3b introduced by the Maastricht Treaty has serious limitations which detract from such limited practical effect as the doctrine of subsidiarity might otherwise have had.

(3) The guidelines adopted at the Birmingham and Edinburgh summits have done nothing effective to remedy the deficiencies present in Article 3b of the Treaty text. They must be regarded essentially as a window-dressing exercise.

(4) The institutions which are charged with interpreting that doctrine will not give it any effective weight unless they are fundamentally reformed.

The doctrine of "subsidiarity" is therefore, without profound institutional reform or changes of attitude or both, virtually worthless as a protection against further unwanted expansion of the European laws and institutions into further aspects of national life. It may, in fact, be worse than worthless if, by giving an illusion of protection, it encourages agreement to measures which would not otherwise be agreed to.

5.3 Maastricht and "intergovernmentalism"

Most areas of the Maastricht Treaty consist of amendments to the existing EEC Treaty, the Treaty of Rome. However, in two important areas, the Maastricht Treaty contains new provisions of its own outside the structure of the existing Treaty of Rome. These are Title V on the common foreign and security policy of the European Union, and Title VI on justice and home affairs.

The fact that these provisions are outside the Treaty of Rome has been hailed by the British Government as an indication that the Maastricht Treaty has checked the centralising tendency of the European Communities. This claim was put as follows by the Prime Minister in his Conservative Party Conference speech on 9th October 1992:

"There is one great prize in the Treaty. For the first time we have reached agreement on developing the community involuntary co-operation between independent nation states. That means outside the Treaty of Rome; outside the jurisdiction of the European Court; outside the competence of the European Commission. We have wanted this principle established for years. And we now have it in the Treaty I agreed. It is time the distortions were put to one side. It is time to return the debate to reality and away from myth."

In his list of Commission portfolios announced on 22nd December 1992, Mr Delors gave a portfolio on the common foreign and security policy to Mr Hans van den Broek, former Dutch foreign minister, and a portfolio on justice and home affairs to Mr Padraig Flynn. It is curious to see the better part of the time of two full time Commissioners being devoted to matters which are, according to the Prime Minister, outside the Commission's competence. However, examination of the Maastricht Treaty text shows that the Commission is to be "fully associated with the work carried out" in both the foreign (Article J.9) and home affairs (Article K.4(2)), and has a right to draft and propose legislation on immigration policy, drug addiction and international fraud, and civil judicial co-operation.

At present there is co-operation on certain foreign policy areas between European countries under the Single European Act. The Maastricht Treaty sets up machinery for the common foreign and security policy of the new European Union. This, unlike the co-operation in limited areas under the present Single European Act, is to cover "all areas of foreign and security policy" (Article J.1(1)), and "shall include all questions related to the security of the Union, including the eventual framing of a common defence policy" (Article J.4(1)).

All Member States are required to support the policy decided by the Council of Ministers "actively and unreservedly", and to "refrain from any action which is contrary to the interests of the Union" (Article J.1(4)).

The Treaty says that this policy "might in time lead to a common defence" (joint armed forces). The present Western European Union is to be integrated into the common defence policy of the new European Union.

Because of the "intergovernmental" structure of this part of the Treaty, primary responsibility for co-ordinating the Union's foreign policy is supposed to lie with the President: each country is President in rotation for a 6-month term. However, in view of the Commission's involvement this may turn out to be more myth than reality. The contest for influence between a rotating 6-month Presidency and a permanent Commission may prove unequal.

From a Federalist perspective, the "intergovernmental" machinery of the foreign and security policy may slow down, but does not prevent, its eventual incorporation fully into the machinery of the European Community. It is just a stepping stone on the way.

Under the Justice and Home Affairs title of the Maastricht Treaty, immigration policy, asylum policy and border controls on the external frontiers of the European Union are to be matters of common interest. The issue of visas to nationals from outside the Union is to be decided by the Council of Ministers, from 1996 by a majority vote; these visa control measures coming immediately within the Treaty of Rome under new Article 100c.

Other matters covered are judicial co-operation in civil and criminal matters, and police co-operation through a new body (Europol) against drug trafficking, terrorism, international frauds and other serious international crimes.

Once common policies are agreed in these fields, there are two alternative mechanisms for implementing them. They may be put into force by a special convention between member states (which may stipulate that the ECJ shall have power to interpret them), or they may simply be adopted as Community measures under Article 100c of the Treaty of Rome.

So, co-operation in the field of justice and home affairs remains "intergovernmental" only while the legislation is not yet agreed. Once legislation is agreed, it appears that it will be enforceable, and subject to interpretation by the ECJ, in the same way as other parts of Community law.

Properly analysed, Title VI of the Maastricht Treaty is not a bulwark of intergovernmental co-operation against the expansion of the powers of the Commission and the other Community institutions, so much as a conveyor belt for the progressive addition of powers in this field to those institutions.

When the provisions of these two so-called "intergovernmental" parts of the Treaty are examined, it can be seen that the claim that they represent "decentralisation" bears no relation to reality.

5.4 Citizenship of the European Union

The Maastricht Treaty introduces a new concept to the European Communities: that of citizenship of the European Union. Article 8 confers this citizenship on every person holding the nationality of a member state. It states that "Citizens of the Union shall enjoy the rights conferred by this Treaty and shall be subject to the duties imposed thereby."

The concept of citizenship of the European Union contains symbolism of enormous power. The practical rights to be given to citizens of the

Union could instead have been conferred on a reciprocal basis on citizens of other member states, as under the present Community Treaties. However, this symbolic and emotive concept has been introduced, and deliberately introduced, when it is not required in order to achieve the practical purposes of the Treaty. What is the purpose of this symbolism?

The introduction of the notion of European citizenship was proposed by Mr Felipe Gonzalez, Spanish Prime Minister, and was endorsed by the Commission and others. The Commission considered that the object of this notion would be "to encourage a feeling of involvement in European integration."[81]

The Commission proposed that European citizens should have rights of free residence and movement, and to vote in local and European Parliament elections. These are duly incorporated into the Maastricht Treaty. The Commission further proposed:

"the setting of targets for the definition of the individual's civic, economic and social rights at a later stage."

The introduction of the concept of European citizenship, together with an initial bundle of rights, can be seen to be the start of a far larger project under which the Community would progressively define the "civic, economic and social rights and obligations"[82] of the individual. In other words, the Community would take over and define the key aspects of the individual's relationship with the state: something which is at the core of the existence of the nation state.

That establishment of European citizenship is a progressive process which can be seen from the new Article 8e, which lays down a 3-yearly cycle of review of the rights of European citizenship. The Council of Ministers is empowered "to strengthen or add to" the rights already laid down.

The Treaty also refers to European citizens having "duties" under the Treaty (Article 8(2)). These duties are nowhere expressly defined and will presumably be deduced by a process of interpretation by the European Court.

It has been stated that European citizenship is additional to national citizenship, and does not deprive anyone of their own national citizenship. But many British citizens are citizens of London, say, or Birmingham, as well. Which citizenship is of most importance? The important question is not extinction of national citizenship, but rather the relative balance, now and in the future, between the significance of national and European citizenships. Will national citizenship become progressively downgraded in its importance?

5.5 Monetary Union and the UK's "opt-out"

One of the main objects of the Maastricht Treaty on European Union is the creation of a single European currency, the ECU, which is intended to replace the national currencies of Member States. The United Kingdom has negotiated an "opt-out" from the European single currency, and it is widely assumed that this opt-out means that the monetary union obligations in the Maastricht Treaty are not of great importance unless and until the UK takes a decision to "opt in" to the single currency.

However, the "opt-out" relates only to the third or final stage of monetary union. The UK is bound to participate in stages 1 and 2 of monetary union. Further, the Treaty contains obligations regarding the conduct of UK exchange rate and monetary policy during Stage 3 even if the pound then remains a separate currency "opted out" of final currency union. How much freedom of action will we retain as regards the UK's future exchange rate and monetary policy? In particular, would it be compatible with the Treaty to stay out of the ERM and float for an indefinite period, should that be judged to be in the best interests of the United Kingdom?

Stages 1 and 2 of monetary union envisage the progressive "convergence" of the economies of the Member States, leading up to the third and final stage when the new European single currency will be introduced. As part of the process of convergence, it is envisaged that Member States will seek to maintain their currencies in the narrow bands of the Exchange Rate Mechanism ("ERM") and strive to avoid devaluation.[83]

At the start of Stage 3 (at the latest on 1st January 1999), a European Central Bank will issue the new single currency. It will replace the currencies of those Member States who satisfy the "convergence criteria" set out in Article 109j of the Treaty. These convergence criteria are low inflation, a low public sector deficit and, most crucially, staying in ERM narrow bands for at least 2 years without a devaluation.

Member States who do not satisfy the criteria will retain their own currencies. Under the Treaty they will have a "derogation" from full monetary union. It is envisaged that these Member States will continue to strive to achieve the "convergence criteria": as and when they do so, their derogations will be removed and they will join the ECU block. In the meantime, they are excluded from voting rights in the operation of the European Central Bank and ECU monetary and interest rate policy.

The effect of the United Kingdom's "opt-out" is that we are obliged to take part in Stages 1 and 2 of monetary union, but need not take part in Stage 3 (abolition of sterling and its replacement by the ECU) unless we opt to do so. Once Stage 3 is in force, the UK will be treated in the same way as a Member State with a "derogation".

National interest versus "common interest": Each member state is bound, so long as it retains its own currency, to "treat its exchange rate policy as a matter of common interest".[84] This obligation applies both during stages 1 and 2, and after the start of stage 3 to any remaining "derogated" currencies including sterling.

According to orthodox principles of interpretation of Community law, the scope of this obligation must be ascertained from its place in the structure of the Treaty and from the Treaty objectives which it is designed to further. Plainly, it imposes a duty over and above that of pursuing an exchange rate policy solely in the national interest.

The concept of "common interest" as regards exchange rate policy is not academic or unimportant. In his speech to the Conservative Party Conference on 8th October 1992, the Chancellor of the Exchequer urged the British car industry to take advantage of the depreciation of the sterling exchange rate by exporting vigorously to Continental markets. The increased competitiveness of British industry resulting from sterling devaluation will necessarily cause concern to Continental car manufacturers, and indeed in other industries as well. There are demands that the UK should return to the ERM as soon as possible.

What if the United Kingdom, once Maastricht is in force, wishes to continue floating the exchange rate for the time being or for an indefinite period? There is then likely to be a pattern of steadily mounting pressure from other Member States, followed by Commission representations that the UK's stance prejudices the purposes of the Treaty. During Stage 2, the European Monetary Institute is likely to recommend the UK's return to the ERM under its powers to make recommendations regarding the exchange rate policies of individual member states.[85]

A reference by the Commission to the European Court of Justice ("ECJ") would ultimately become likely if the UK were to remain obdurate in the indefinite pursuit of a floating exchange rate policy. The ECJ would be likely to hold that a policy on the part of the UK of indefinitely remaining outside the ERM is contrary to the Treaty. In such circumstances, the United Kingdom would be avowedly pursuing an exchange rate policy based on its own national interest rather than treating it as a matter of "common interest" as required by Article 109m.

The whole structure of Stages 1 and 2 monetary union presupposes that Member States are striving towards achievement of the convergence criteria, including more tightly aligned parities. Although the UK has opted out of the final stage 3 objective of currency merger, it has not opted out of the objective of exchange rate convergence. It is an important aspect of the single market as envisaged by the scheme of the Treaty that there should be currency stability as far as possible across the whole market, and the UK's conduct would be considered by the ECJ as imperiling the attainment of that central Treaty objective.

It is of course true that the Treaty contemplates that some Member States may fail to achieve the convergence criteria, hence "derogation" for those who fail. It does not follow that Member States have no **obligation to try**. The Treaty is framed to a large extent in terms of policy objectives.

What if the UK were to pursue a stated policy of intending to return to the ERM when conditions allow, but were to persist for an indefinite period in saying that conditions were unsuitable? This policy might work for a limited period, at the expense of creating suspicion, mistrust and ill-will amongst our Community partners. It could not be expected to work for long.

During Stage 3, the obligation to maintain a stable parity against the ECU for opted out and "derogated" currencies would if anything be even greater. Countries which had entered into the ECU block, such as, say, France, would have lost the possibility of ever devaluing against Germany. They would be likely to complain vociferously if their industries were subjected to intense UK competition as a result of a fluctuating sterling exchange rate.

The dubious benefits of the opt-out: The UK's position, if opted out of Stage 3 monetary union, would be quite invidious. The UK would then have a Treaty obligation to seek to maintain a narrow band parity against the ECU block. However, the UK would be excluded from voting on the Governing Council which takes interest rate decisions for the ECU currency. The UK would be obliged to follow ECU interest rates in order to maintain its parity, but would have no say in setting them. The UK "opt-out" from Stage 3 is therefore so unattractive that it must be queried whether it can be regarded as anything more than an attempt at window dressing.

The choice is either not to ratify Maastricht, or the inevitable road to full monetary union: the "opt-out" is not a real option.

5.6 Maastricht and the Social Charter

The Prime Minister and the Government were hailed for their achievement at the Maastricht Summit in December 1991 in reaching an agreement with the other Member States which permitted the United Kingdom to "opt-out" of the Social Charter.

In fact, the mechanism adopted was that certain provisions popularly known as the "Social Charter" were, by a Protocol to the Maastricht Treaty, incorporated in a separate agreement concluded by all the

Member States except Britain. This is called the "Agreement on Social Policy". It primarily relates to workplace and trade union rights.

There is little doubt that the Social Charter is profoundly antipathetic to the principles and values which the Conservatives have been seeking to achieve in 12 years of Conservative government. If implemented, it would seriously undermine those achievements.

If the Labour party were to win a general election victory, it would be free to introduce such measures. However, a newly elected Labour government would be subject to being removed, and its policies reversed, after 5 years if that were the democratic verdict of the British people. The difference with the European Social Charter is that once implemented it cannot be reversed or repealed by any exercise of the democratic will of the British people, short of the United Kingdom leaving the European Communities or a totally fundamental change in our relationship with it.

The hard question must therefore be asked: Has the British Government succeeded in its objectives by securing the hiving-off of the Social Agreement provisions from the main Maastricht Treaty?

It must be appreciated that this hiving-off only relates to the new Social Agreement provisions and does not relate to the existing provisions of the Treaty of Rome (as amended by the Single European Act) dealing with social matters. The United Kingdom is still bound by these, and by regulations and directives made under them. Furthermore, other provisions of the Treaty, such as those dealing with single market measures, may be employed indirectly to regulate social matters.

The most notable provisions of the Treaty of Rome in this context are Article 118a dealing with health and safety at work; and Article 100a which deals with single market measures. Both of these Articles were inserted into the Treaty by the Single European Act, and both require only a qualified majority, rather than a unanimous, vote in the Council of Ministers for the adoption of regulations or directives under them. To what extent can these provisions be used, and are they likely to be used, to sidestep the exclusion of the United Kingdom from the Social Charter?

First, as regards motivation. Free market economists in Britain would like to see British industry in a position to compete in the single market without the anti-competitive shackles of the Social Charter. By the same token, Member States who are adopting the Social Charter as part of their own laws will be loath to see their industries exposed to competition in the single market from British companies which are not subject to its costs and disadvantages. Quite apart from and on top of those considerations, there is a palpable desire in some quarters to deprive Britain of the fruits of this particular victory against the dream of European Union. One must expect a clear willingness on the part of the European institutions and the majority of other Member States to try to undermine as far as possible the United Kingdom's exclusion from the Social Charter, and to achieve the same results as the Social Charter through other Treaty mechanisms.

This is already happening in one important area: the Social Charter's 48 hour working week is re-appearing in another guise as a draft "health and safety" directive under Article 118a of the Treaty. The ultimate outcome of this battle is not clear at the time of writing, although it appears that the United Kingdom has accepted the principle of Community regulation of working hours under this guise in return for concessions of detail.

This is a dangerous concession if it is correctly reported; since, once the principle is accepted, even if the actual provisions are acceptable, the way is open for future European regulation of this area in a more extensive, detailed and restrictive way. Furthermore, this would appear to be just the first in a long series of potential measures which, taken collectively, threaten almost entirely to undermine the Maastricht Treaty's exclusion of the United Kingdom from the Social Charter.

If a measure is introduced as, say, a single market measure, and voted through by a majority against the wishes of the United Kingdom, the United Kingdom then has only one further recourse left: to challenge the validity of the directive or regulation concerned before the European Court of Justice. How will that Court decide? From the nature of that Court's jurisprudence described above, there is little room for confidence that it would come to a decision favourable to the United Kingdom.

Some indication of the Court's likely attitude can be gleaned from the words of part of its judgment in the *Defrenne* sex equality case:

"First, in the light of the different stages of the development of social legislation in the various Member States, the aim of Article 119 is to avoid a situation in which undertakings established in States which have actually implemented the principle of equal pay have suffered a competitive disadvantage in intra-Community competition as compared with undertakings established in States which have not yet eliminated discrimination against women workers as regards pay."[86]

This reasoning could obviously justify the adoption of a wide range of "Social Charter" measures under internal market majority vote powers, on the alleged grounds of rectifying a competitive disadvantage.

It must be noted that in the event of such a Court decision against the United Kingdom, there is then, as things stand, no further constitutional line of defence against the direct implementation of the measure by the courts of the United Kingdom: they are obliged, by section 3(1) of the European Communities Act 1972, to apply Community law "in accordance with the principles laid down by and any relevant decision of the European Court" whether or not those would coincide with their own view of the meaning of the Treaty provisions concerned.

The conclusion must be that the hiving-off of the Social Charter from the Maastricht Treaty in fact gives limited protection for the United Kingdom against circumvention, given the current state of mind and institutional trends of the European institutions.

Chapter 6

The Way Ahead

6.1 Protecting the British Constitution

It has been noted above that the present arrangements for the incorporation of Community law into United Kingdom law leave the United Kingdom peculiarly vulnerable to unexpectedly wide interpretations of Community law. There is even, as noted in Chapter 2.2 above, a residual doubt as to whether Parliament now has, under our law, the ultimate power to revoke Community law in the United Kingdom if it ever wished to do so. The Bill currently before Parliament to ratify the Maastricht Treaty does not alter the constitutional position established by the European Communities Act 1972: it merely amends that Act to add the Maastricht Treaty to the list of Treaties which are to form part of "Community law".

Other Member States have written constitutions which inherently place bounds upon the extent to which Community law may intrude into their constitutional arrangements. The constitution of the United Kingdom, being unwritten, imposes no such bounds.

Other Member States do have constitutional structures which effectively preserve their national interests even if there is a conflict with Community law.[87]

The most important instance when a Member State has defied Community rules to safeguard what it sees as its essential national interests was the action of non-co-operation taken by President de Gaulle in 1965. This led in January 1966 to the Luxembourg Accords where it was agreed that decisions of the Council of Ministers should, even where the Treaty provides for majority voting, be reached by unanimous agreement where the very important interests of a Member State are involved.

The legal status of the Luxembourg Accords is somewhat uncertain, since they are not formally embodied in any Treaty provision or comparable measure.[88]

The likely potential for future conflict in the Community, in fields such as the circumvention of the United Kingdom's Social Charter opt-out or the desire of the United Kingdom to maintain its border controls, leads strongly to the desirability of the implementation of measures in domestic law (irrespective of what may happen at Community level) to clarify the status of Community law in the United Kingdom. The measures which could be taken are fairly straightforward, involving the amendment of sections 2 and 3 of the European Communities Act 1972 to enact the following:

Supremacy of Parliament: The ultimate supremacy of Parliament over all Community law, in other words the ultimate right of Parliament by express provision to that effect to abrogate in whole or in part or to vary the operation of Community law as part of the law of the United Kingdom, should be expressly laid down.

Conflicts between Acts of Parliament and Community law: The rules relating to conflicts between Community law and Acts of Parliament, if they unintentionally arise, should be expressly spelled out. Instead of it being left to the courts to suspend or disapply Acts of Parliament on an interim basis, as in the *Factortame* case, a procedure should be substituted whereby a court in such a situation would refer the matter to the Lord President of the Council who would then have power to propose for Parliamentary approval an Order in Council dealing with any necessary suspension of an Act and making alternative provision in the meantime.

Reserve list of protected matters: To guard against unexpectedly wide interpretations of Community law, there should be an express list of reserved matters which no Community law should, under the law of the United Kingdom, be allowed to affect. That list would include the constitution and procedure of Parliament and the procedure for election to it; the relationship of government, Parliament and the Courts; the defence, war and security powers of the United Kingdom; and other central constitutional matters.

Reserve Powers: Given the likely nature of the conflict over border controls and over the "back door Social Charter", the Government would be wise to equip itself with reserve powers, exercisable by Order in Council, to render specified decisions or acts of Community institutions of no effect under the laws of the United Kingdom.

In the case of the proposed reserve powers, it might be queried whether such a provision could potentially bring the United Kingdom into conflict with Community law. It must be remembered that other Member States have not been averse to coming into conflict with Community law when it has suited them to do so: the most important occasion was de Gaulle in 1965 in the clash which led to the Luxembourg compromise. Such a reserve power merely offers the potential to lift an essentially political dispute from the level of the Courts, who are not best equipped to deal with it, to the political plane of relations between states where it belongs.

It must also be remembered that Community law and international law are not necessarily the same thing. If, for instance, the ECJ were to find that the "Declaration" relating to anti-immigration and anti-terrorism measures annexed to the Single European Act (as quoted previously) had no force as part of Community law, the UK might wish to argue that it amounted effectively to such a breach regarding its expectations at the time of signing of the Single European Act, on a matter of vital national interest, that it ought not to be obliged to comply.

The Member States' submission to the interpretative powers of the ECJ is based upon the assumption that those powers will be exercised properly and judicially and within the limits laid down by the Treaties. It is, at the very least, arguable that some decisions of the ECJ have gone beyond those limits and accordingly are not binding on Member States as a matter of international law.

As well as being a useful weapon in the event of back door attempts to introduce the Social Charter, such reserve powers could, by their very existence, deter both other Member States and the Commission from a rash course of conflict with the United Kingdom which would amount to depriving the United Kingdom of what it believed in good faith that it had secured at Maastricht in December 1991.

6.2 "Ever closer union" and the 1996 Treaty revision

"From time to time we hear objections that the Maastricht treaty does not give a clear enough picture of what tomorrow's Europe should actually look like. This was not the aim of the treaty, nor could it be. Maastricht was an interim step, albeit an important one, on the road to European Union.

The parts of the treaty dealing with political union are just as important as those concerning economic and monetary union... An economic union will survive only if it is based on a political union."

Chancellor Helmut Kohl, Financial Times, 4th January 1993

As already noted in section 4.3 above, the concept of "ever closer union" appeared in the preamble to the original Rome Treaty. Maastricht moves this commitment into the substantive Treaty text, in Article A, as follows:

"This Treaty marks a new stage in the process of creating an ever closer union among the peoples of Europe, in which decisions are taken as closely as possible to the citizen."

The Maastricht Treaty must be considered not only in terms of the powers which it now confers upon the European Community, but also in terms of its future development. It is difficult to read the actual Treaty text without reacting to claims that the Treaty is "decentralising" or "checks the trend towards a Federal super state" without disbelief, or indeed complete bewilderment.

Not only does the Treaty confer additional powers on the European Community, and upon the new European Union, but it also contains clear and explicit commitments to expand on and add to those powers. The main means by which this is to be done is by a Treaty revision conference to be convened in 1996.[89]

The main task of this conference is set out in Article B:

"... to maintain in full the 'acquis communautaire' and build on it with a view to considering, through the procedure referred to in Article N(2), to what extent the policies and forms of co-operation introduced by this

Treaty may need to be revised with the aim of ensuring the effectiveness of the mechanisms and institutions of the Community."

What is the *"acquis communautaire"* ? The word *acquis* is the past participle of the verb *acquerir*, which means to acquire, win, or gain. The word *acquis* is used in the phrases *acquis fait*, which means established or accepted, and in *il est maintenant acquis que ...* , meaning "it has now been established or accepted that ... " The word is used in the field of legal rights: *ce droit nous est acquis*, meaning "we have now established this right as ours".

It is this latter meaning which is closest to its meaning in the phrase *"acquis communautaire"*: this means the corpus of powers, privileges and abilities to act which has been built up by the Community whether through express provisions of the Treaties, formal legislative measures taken under them, or more subtly through custom and practice, particularly through steps taken at both formal and informal meetings and discussions.

This part of the Maastricht Treaty therefore involves an acceptance of irreversibility. Since nothing must be taken away or removed from the *"acquis communautaire"*, it must forever be built on or added to. This is another expression of the doctrine of the "occupied field", already developed by the ECJ, whereby, once the Community has legislated in a field, the Member States are precluded from entering.[90]

In addition to the general commitment to revise the Treaty to ensure the "effectiveness" of the Community, there are specific commitments to consider the addition to the Treaty of Rome of new Titles on energy, civil protection and tourism,[91] and to review the development of the common defence policy in the light of the 1998 expiry date of the Brussels Treaty which establishes the Western European Union. This presumably means that after then the common defence policy will be taken fully in-house by the European Union, rather than being operated through the WEU.

The Maastricht Treaty therefore contains express commitments both general and particular to the further expansion in 1996 of the powers of the European Community and the European Union. It can be argued that actual agreement to the revised Treaty will require unanimous consent. But past history has repeatedly shown that it is in practice difficult or impossible to use the withholding of unanimous consent to block a new policy or initiative, once there has been agreement in principle that such a new policy will take place.

Such conduct evokes accusations of bad faith, anger, and retaliatory measures in other aspects of Community negotiations where the support of other states is needed in order to achieve objectives which we seek.

So called "Euro-waffle" of this kind does have both legal force and real political force. The strong presumptions built into the Maastricht Treaty regarding the 1996 revision are likely in large measure to condition the direction and outcome of that Treaty revision.

6.3 What happens if Maastricht is not ratified?

If Maastricht is not ratified by the UK, the EEC will still be there. There is very little in the Maastricht Treaty which has to do with the single market. The Treaty of Rome and the Single European Act, which lay down the single market, would continue in force as they stand at present.[92]

There is no legal power to compel a Member State to agree to Treaty changes it does not want, or to threaten it with expulsion if it does not agree. Only if other Member States were to rip up their existing Treaty obligations in a fit of pique would the single market come to an end – unthinkable, and anyway contrary to their interests since the UK buys more goods and services from the rest of the Community than they do from us. The UK tax payer and consumer saves the common agricultural policy from bankruptcy.

Could a group of Member States, frustrated by non-ratification of Maastricht by Denmark and/or the UK, go ahead by themselves? It is not possible to bring the Maastricht Treaty into force for some Member States only. In theory, it might be possible for a group of Member States to agree among themselves a new Treaty implementing some of the policies in the Maastricht Treaty. There would be extreme political difficulties in doing so, given the high and rising levels of opposition to Maastricht in France and Germany, as an even more federalising Treaty would face even more opposition. Sporadic talk of a new Treaty is probably a mixture of pipe dreams and sabre rattling by frustrated Federalists.

Even if an inner core group were to go ahead with a new Treaty, this would leave Member States that did not join the new block outside the new group, but inside the internal market under the existing Treaty of Rome and Single European Act. The industries of those outside would then be able to compete without being subject to the interventionist regulations of Maastricht, or bearing the costs of the large increases in Community spending which Maastricht involves.

6.4 Promoting a Europe of Nation States

It is now time to some extent to move beyond the task of analysing the current path of development of the European Communities, and to discuss objectives. To someone who firmly believes in the onward progression of the European Communities into a single super-State, nothing in the foregoing discussion of the behaviour and attributes of the Community institutions, or the effects of the Maastricht Treaty, will be unwelcome.

If, as I believe is the wish of the vast majority of the British public, we seek to promote a harmonious Europe but essentially a Europe of nation states, it is apparent that there are many aspects of the present functioning of the European Communities and of the structure and culture of its institutions which militate against achieving those objectives.

Thus, we always seem to find ourselves in the position of merely slowing down, watering down or delaying what is presented as an inevitable process of ever further European integration. In a way, the present position in Europe resembles that in the United Kingdom before the election of Mrs Thatcher's government in 1979, when it was thought that the "ratchet effect" would lead inevitably to more and more socialism, with intervals of Conservative government merely slowing down or even stopping, but never reversing, the inevitable progress of the ratchet. Do we now face an inevitable European ratchet effect?

The only way in which we can hope not to do so is to define our own clear positive objectives for the future development of the Community, rather than merely acting as clogs slowing down progress to objectives defined by other people. The objectives we would wish to set may at present be far away from the current "political realities" of the European Community: but Mrs Thatcher's government showed that political realities can change or be changed. The starting point is to clearly define our own objectives, and thereafter seek to persuade others to subscribe to those objectives.

If, as I believe it is, our objective is a Europe of nation states, then our first task should be to seek that that objective is clearly stated in the Treaties. There should be no presumption that, as and when the Community institutions have completely expanded into their current fields of activity, they should automatically search to expand into ever wider fields of national life. Instead, the Treaty should state the objective of progressive reduction of the role of the European Communities and the Community institutions as regards their fields of activities, and indeed recognition for the disparate roles of member states within fields occupied by the Community institutions.

In drafting terms, this would mean that, if and when the Treaty is next revised, we should ask that the reference in the first preamble to the Treaty of Rome (and in Article A of Maastricht if it is ratified) to "an ever closer union among the peoples of Europe" should be deleted and replaced by an appropriate recognition of Europe as consisting of independent nation states closely co-operating for their mutual benefit in clearly defined areas.

We should have a positive plan for the reform of the European institutions, which in their present form have an inbuilt tendency to promote European centralism, whatever Treaty wordings may purport to contain them. The most important institution to reform is the Court. It is incapable, as demonstrated above, of acting as an impartial body where the respective competence of the European institutions and the Member States is at issue. What is needed is, on important questions on the scope of Treaty powers, a further appeal above the European Court of Justice to a European Constitutional Court consisting of judges convened *ad hoc* from the higher courts of the

Member States. Such a court would be far less likely to become committed to a particular viewpoint about the desirability of ever expanding European institutions than the presently constituted ECJ.

The other important body which needs reform, and which perhaps is most difficult to reform, is the Commission. A start would be to abolish the office of President of the Commission, since this post acts both as a focus for an undesirable concentration of powers and an encouragement to the egotistical tendencies of its incumbent.[93] The task of chairing the Commission could then pass in strict rotation to its members in the same way as the Presidency of the Council of Ministers.

Any worthwhile reform of the Commission will have to end the present practice of giving to each Commissioner an individual portfolio. Successive enlargement of the Communities has resulted in a Commission which originally consisted of 9 members now consisting of 17, with each one having to be found a job. This practice will become even more undesirable if the EEC is enlarged further. The political problem will be that each Member State will want some representation on the Commission. Perhaps the only solution is to convert the Commission to a larger non-executive body which is reported to by civil servants who are heads of departments. The way is then open for the wholesale abolition of those departments of the Commission which are themselves a standing affront to the principle of "subsidiarity".

An alternative, more radical, solution, might be the division of the Commission into a number of smaller separate bodies, one dealing for example with the internal market and external trade, one with agriculture, and one with a radically reduced residue of matters outside either of those headings. If the separate bodies were then located in physically separate European cities, the tendency for centralisation of power would be further reduced.

A logical progression of the "hiving-off" of the Social Agreement at Maastricht would be to seek that all the Social Provisions of the Treaty of Rome were separated out into a separate Treaty which would be adhered to by the parties to the Maastricht Social Agreement. This, coupled with explicit Treaty limitations on the intrusion of internal market powers into the social field, would end or at least substantially reduce the present dangers of the indirect circumvention of the United Kingdom's opt-out from the Social Charter. The institutional corollary of this could be the hiving-off of the social affairs functions of the Commission to a separate body answerable to those Member States alone.

We should press for far clearer delimitations of Community powers. For example, the single market powers should be limited to powers to **remove obstacles to trade**. They should not be drafted in such a way that they can be argued to justify the compulsory imposition of burdens on industry, upon the specious grounds that fair competition requires the imposition of equal social burdens on employers in all Member States.

We should seek the wholesale abolition of other powers. Why, for example, should health and safety at work be a matter for European regulation at all? Practices permitted in one Member State may be considered unacceptably dangerous in another Member State, but what business is it of the latter?

Another area which calls out for wholesale abolition of European powers is that of environment: apart from those aspects of environmental protection which may affect other Member States such as smoke emissions or discharges into the sea, what case is there for environmental regulation at European level? Whether it is right or wrong to build a motorway through Twyford Down near Winchester, what concern is it of other Member States, and how are we concerned about the line of motorways in Belgium?

It is clear that there is much to be done in formulating a positive programme of reform for the European Communities. The fact that the road from formulating those proposals to their ultimate implementation may well be long drawn out and difficult, is not a reason for not starting that task: rather the contrary.

Notes

1   Case 26/62: *Van Gend en Loos v. Nederlandse Administratie der Belastingen* [1963] ECR 1 at 12.

2   Article G.

3   *Variola SPA v. Italian Finance Ministry* [1973] ECR 981 at 992 para [15].

4   Lasok and Bridge, "Law and Institutions of the European Communities" 5th Ed., Ch 5.

5   Germany, France, Italy and the UK have 10 votes each; Spain has 8; Belgium, Greece, Netherlands and Portugal have 5; Denmark and Ireland have 3; Luxembourg 2. A majority of 54 votes out of the available 78 is needed: Treaty of Rome, Article 148(2).

6   "The Commission is, at one and the same time, the guardian of the Treaties and the motive force of integration ... " Statement by the President of the Commission to the European Parliament, 15 Sept 1970.

7   Treaty of Rome, Article 155.

8   Changed from "European Assembly" to "European Parliament" by the Single European Act.

9   Article 171 of the Treaty of Rome, as amended by Maastricht.

10   *Amministrzione delle Finanze v. Simmenthal Spa* [1978] ECR 629 at 644.

11   *Internationale Handelsgesellschaft v. Einfuhr und Vorratsstelle Getreide* [1970] ECR 1125 at 1134.

12   *H.P. Bulmer Ltd v. Bollinger SA* [1974] 2 CMLR 91 at 111. Lord Denning has in fact recently said that he would like to amend this quotation to read: "No longer is European law an incoming tide flowing up the estuaries of England. It is now like a tidal wave bringing down our sea walls and flowing inland over our fields and houses – to the dismay of all..." Introduction to Gavin Smith, The ECJ: Judges or Policy Makers?

13   E.g. the United States, where Treaties upon ratification by a two-thirds majority of the Senate become part of the "supreme law of the land".

14   JDB Mitchell, (1980) 11 Cambrian Law Review 69.

15   See Lord Bridge in *R. v. Secretary of State for Transport ex p. Factortame Ltd* [1990] 2 AC 85 at 140B-D. It was put by Hoffmann J in *Stoke-on-Trent v. B & Q* [1990] 3 CMLR 31 at 34 as follows: "The Treaty of Rome is the supreme law of this country, taking precedence over Acts of Parliament. Our entry into the Community meant that (subject to our undoubted but probably theoretical right to withdraw from the Community altogether) Parliament surrendered its sovereign right to legislate contrary to the Treaty on the matters of social and economic policy which it regulated."

16   [1976] ECR 455.

17   At p. 476.

18   At p. 481, para [75].

19   Save for a power to make its own rules of procedure: Article 188(3).

20   *Defrenne v. SABENA* [1978] ECR 1365. The *SABENA* case was referred to the ECJ twice.

21   At p. 1378.

22   [1990] 3 CMLR 513.

23   At p. 559.

24   [1975] OJ L45/19.

25   [1976] OJ L39/40.

26   [1979] OJ L6/24.

27   [1986] OJ L225/40.

28   [1976] ECR 455 at 473, para [20].

29   Council Regulation 170/83.

30   See *R v. MAFF, Ex p. Agegate* Case 3/87.

31   [1989] 2 CMLR 353

32   1989] 2 CMLR 353

33   [1990] 2 AC 85.

34   [1990] AC 85 at 142G-143B.

35   Case 213/89; [1990] 3 CMLR 1 at 30.

36   [1990] 3 CMLR 375.

37 Case C-221/89, *The Times* 16 Sept 1991.

38 [1990] 3 CMLR 31.

39 [1974] ECR 837.

40 *Rewe-Zentral AG* [1979] ECR 649.

41 *Torfaen v. B & Q* [1990] 1 CMLR 337.

42 At p. 364.

43 *Stoke on Trent City Council v. B & Q PLC* [1990] 3 CMLR 31.

44 Case C-169/91, reported in *The Times*, 17 Dec 1992.

45 *Torfaen* [1990] 1 CMLR 337 at 364, para [14].

46 Evening Standard, 14 May 1992.

47 At page 24, in answer to the question "Will Britain be able to maintain frontier controls?"

48 [1964] ECR 585 at 594.

49 E *C Commission v. Italy* [1972] ECR 527.

50 For a comprehensive, and lucid, analysis of the concept of sovereignty and the various ways in which the word is used and misused, see "Sense on Sovereignty", Noel Malcolm, Centre for Policy Studies.

51 For discussion of this point under the law of the United Kingdom, see 2.2 previously.

52 For some examples of this use of the word, see Noel Malcolm, op.cit., pp. 6 to 9.

53 For the powers of the Court see Treaty of Rome, Articles 173 and 177.

54 Treaty of Rome, Article 165.

55 Treaty of Rome, Article 167.

56 [1960] ECR 355, at 374.

57 See Schermers, H, "The European Court of Justice: Promoter of European Integration" 22 AJCL (1974) pp. 459 et seq.

58 Advocate-General Lagrange in *Hoogovens v. High Authority* [1963] CMLR 73 at 85, 86.

59 *Internationale Handelsgesellschaft GmbH v. Einfuhr-und-Vorratsstelle* [1970] ECR 1125 at 1146.

60 See *Star Fruit Co SA v. EC Commission* [1990] 1 CMLR 733.

61 [1974] ECR 1337; concerned directive 64/221 on the right of entry of workers from other Member States; following *Grad v. Finanzamt Traunstein* [1970] ECR 825 at 837.

62 [1990] 2 CMLR 833.

63 Listed at [1990] 2 CMLR 857 para [19].

64 [1990] 2 CMLR 43 at 856 para [16].

65 [1963] ECR 1 at 12.

66 [1976] ECR 455 at 472.

67 As reported by The Times, front page, 3 Nov 1992.

68 New Article 103(1) and (2).

69 Article 103(3).

70 Article 103(4).

71 New Article 104c(1).

72 New Article 104c(9) to (11).

73 New Article 109e(5).

74 New Article 137(3).

75 For a historical account, see an article by George Brock in *The Times*, 23 July 1991.

76 For a more extensive analysis of the problems inherent in Article 3b, and for suggestions of steps which could have been taken (but were not) to make subsidiarity work in practice, see "Subsidiarity: How to make it work", Martin Howe, printed as Appendices 4 and 8 to the Interim Report of the House of Commons Foreign Affairs Committee, "Europe after Maastricht", 4 Nov 1992.

77 See *EC Commission v. UK* [1988] 3 CMLR 437.

78 Article 2 as amended by Maastricht Treaty.

79 Lord Mackenzie-Stuart, article in The Times, 11 December 1992.

80 Interview by Lesley White, Sunday Times, 10 May 1992.

81 Commission opinion of 21 November 1990 to the conference drafting the Maastricht Treaty, at p. 79.

82 Commission Opinion, p. 79.

83 Article 109j(2).

84 Article 109m.

85 Article 109f(4).

86 *Defrenne v. SABENA* [1976] ECR 455 at 472 para 9.

87 See the decision of the French Conseil d'Etat in *Minister of the Interior v. Cohn-Bendit* [1980] 1 CMLR 543, which held to be not directly applicable the very directive on free movement of persons which had been held directly applicable by the ECJ in the British *Van Duyn case:* [1974] ECR 1337. See also a similar decision by the German Federal Fiscal Court in *Re VAT Directives* [1982] 1 CMLR 527.

88 See statement of the then Foreign Secretary, Sir Geoffrey Howe, Hansard 1985-86 Vol 96 Col 320.

89 Article N(2).

90 *EC Commission v. UK* [1988] 3 CMLR 437.

91 Declaration on Civil Protection, Energy and Tourism.

92 The Government's response to 20 Questions issued by the Institute of Directors, Q12, was: "The Maastricht Treaty will have absolutely no effect on progress towards the removal of barriers to trade in the European Community. The Maastricht amendments have no effect on the substance of the main Single Market Articles of the Treaty."

93 For example, the draft proposal that the President of the Commission should become "President of Europe" and should permanently preside over the ministers of Member States in the Council of Ministers; reported in *The Sunday Telegraph*, 3rd May 1992.

Nelson & Pollard published the complete text of the Maastricht Treaty under the Title "The Unseen Treaty" in April 1992, ISBN 1-874607-03-6.

At the time of printing, inexpensive copies of the main European treaties are in preparation, to be published as four volumes under the title "The Convoluted Treaties"

The first of these, "The Convoluted Treaties II - Rome 1957 - The European Economic Community" is expected to be available in January 1993. The other titles are to be published shortly after this.

I - Paris 1951 - The European Coal & Steel Community

II - Rome 1957 - The European Economic Community

III - Rome 1957 - The European Atomic Energy Community

IV - The Amending Treaties including the Single European Act

The text of the treaties is also available on computer disc.

Nelson & Pollard Publishing
Folly Bridge Workshops, Thames Street, Oxford OX1 1SU
Telephone : 0865 240048 Facsimile: 0865 792277